STRONG

How God Equipped **11** Ordinary Men

with Extraordinary Power

(and Can Do the Same for You)

CATHERINE PARKS

author of *Empowered*

ILLUSTRATIONS BY CARLO MOLINARI

B&H
PUBLISHING
Nashville, Tennessee

978-1-5359-4635-3

Published by B&H Publishers Group
Nashville, Tennessee

Dewey Decimal Classification: 248.83
Subject Heading: GOD / CHRISTIAN LIFE / BOYS

1 2 3 4 5 6 7 • 22 21 20 19

For Micah, whose name means "Who Is Like God?" Being your mother is one of my greatest joys. May you always remember that He is working in you mightily, helping you to act justly, love mercy, and walk humbly with Him.

Micah 6:8

Acknowledgments

Writing this book convinced me more than ever just how important it is to have fellow travelers supporting us in our endeavors. Each of the men written about in these pages was given encouragers and partners along his way. I want to thank those people who have encouraged me in this project.

B&H envisioned this project and allowed me to bring it to life. Thanks to Holly Spangle, Michelle Burke, and Dave Schroeder for your assistance and brainstorming help. And to Devin Maddox, thanks for recommending the longest Bonhoeffer biography ever written (and the guidance with his story).

Lemanuel Williams, Josh Wester, Erik Parks, and Tom Strode read and gave feedback on these chapters. Thank you for sharpening the work and giving oversight.

The biographers who researched and wrote many of these books made my job possible. Thanks to all those who see the value in bringing history before us and reminding us of our universal need and God's amazing grace.

The T.T.T., my Saturday Bible study girls, and the I.D.K. Society have all been excited to hear about this project, and have cheered me on, as have my parents and in-laws, and many friends.

Special thanks to the men in my life who have embodied so many of these qualities, by the strength and grace of God. Dad, Erik, Aaron, Roger, Kyle, and Peter—God is strong in your weakness. Thank you for pointing your families to Him.

Micah and Sophie, I hope you enjoy reading these stories. More than anything, I hope they show you how incredible God is. You have so many great men in your lives, but they all point us to Jesus as the real hero. Be encouraged that He is working in you!

Acknowledgments

Erik, your humility and quiet strength are a refuge for me. Thank you for loving me, but even more, thank you for loving Him.

Contents

Read This First

I'm so happy you're holding this book! I've spent a long time with the stories of these men, and it's an honor to share those stories with you. But before we start, I want to tell you why this book is called *Strong*.

When you hear the word *strong*, many things might come to mind. Maybe you think of an athlete hitting a home run, or a half-court shot, or an Olympian lifting huge weights. Perhaps an image of a superhero comes to mind. Or maybe you think of someone with mental strength, able to outsmart opponents at tests of skill and strategy. Sometimes we call people strong if they don't cry or yell when they get injured. But this isn't the kind of strength you'll find in this book.

Look at what Paul wrote about strength in his letter to the Colossians when he was telling the people what he prayed for them:

We are asking that you may be filled with the knowledge of his will in all wisdom and spiritual understanding, so that you may walk worthy of the Lord, fully pleasing to him: bearing fruit in every good work and growing in the knowledge of God, being strengthened with all power, according to his glorious might, so that you may have great endurance and patience, joyfully giving thanks to the Father, who has enabled you to share in the saints' inheritance in the light.—Colossians 1:9–12

Look at a few things with me:
First, who strengthens us? God.
With what? All power.
How? According to His glorious might.
Why? So that we may endure and be patient.

This is a different view of strength; one that doesn't require large muscles or athletic ability. There's nothing here about winning fights or never crying. This strength comes from outside of ourselves—from God. And we don't get this strength so that we can win games or show off; this strength helps us do the things God has planned for us, hanging in there and being patient even when things are hard. The purpose of our lives isn't to prove how strong we are; it's to show His strength.

This book tells the stories of eleven men who were all strong in different ways, but every one of them knew his strength had to come from God. Jackie Robinson prayed nightly for strength to endure persecution. George Müller prayed for strength to trust that God would provide what he needed to feed thousands of orphans. Brother Andrew prayed for strength to be bold when bringing Bibles into countries where they were forbidden. Each man in these pages knew his own strength would never be enough; they all needed God's power.

It might be tempting to read these stories and think, *I'll never do any of the big things these guys did.* But that's the great news. When Paul, working under the guidance of the Holy Spirit, wrote those words to the Christians at Colossae, he wasn't writing to "super Christians" who were famous and doing incredible things. He wrote those words to normal people like you and me— people who were just living each day, trying to bring glory to God with their lives.

And the other encouraging thing? Each of the men in this book thought of himself as normal too. These men didn't wake up one morning, thinking, *One day, people are going to write books about how amazing I am.* No, they woke up each day, praying for strength to obey and follow Christ that day. God led them each step of the way, just as He's leading you.

So, as you read about William Carey, Elka of the Wai Wai, George Liele, and all the other men here, remember that the same God who strengthened them can strengthen you too. If you've trusted Christ as your Savior, knowing He died to pay the price for your sin and rose again in victory over death, and if you've given your life to Him, then the Holy Spirit is in you, giving you His power, strengthening you for the things you have to do today. And He'll strengthen you for tomorrow, and the next day, and the next.

My hope is that as you read about these men, you'll be encouraged and inspired by their stories. But more than that, I hope you'll be encouraged by their God. I hope reading about His faithfulness in the lives of these men will encourage you that He's faithfully working in your life too. And I hope that will make you want to know Him more by reading His Word, the Bible, and spending time talking to Him in prayer.

I wrote this book because I wanted my son, Micah, and my nephews, Wolfie, Rafa, Emory, Sullivan, and Leo, to know about these men. But my greater purpose was for all of you to know that God has a plan for your life right where you are and that He will strengthen you to accomplish your purpose each and every day.

Paul's words to another church are my words to you as well: "I am sure of this, that he who started a good work in you will carry it on to completion until the day of Christ Jesus" (Philippians 1:6).

God is faithful—He will strengthen you and help you, just as He did these eleven men!

"I do not care to be remembered as a **WARRIOR** but as one who **HELPED** others to **CHRIST**."

Alvin York
GENEROSITY

Alvin York was born on December 13, 1887, in a cabin his father built on their land in Tennessee. Alvin was the third oldest of his seven brothers and three sisters, and like the others, he had jobs to do around the house and farm. He hauled firewood, carried water, and took care of the babies in the house. When he grew a little bigger, he learned to help his father work in the fields. Because children were needed on the family farms, Alvin and other kids his age didn't go to school except for a few weeks during the summer. He learned to read and write but didn't do much of either one.

Most boys and men in Alvin's community went to shooting matches on Saturdays, where they would pay to compete for prizes like cows and turkeys for their family dinners. They shot long rifles—guns as long as a tall man and weighing at least fifteen pounds. They weren't easy to handle, but they were great for hitting a target, and Alvin was an excellent shooter. One of the contests involved shooting turkeys that were tied behind a log and would occasionally pop their heads up. Alvin had an excellent ability to hit targets (and turkeys), a skill that would one day save his life and the lives of many others.

Other than shooting and farming, Alvin spent a lot of time as a young man drinking and gambling. His father died when he was twenty-four, and Alvin became responsible for the farm and providing for his family. He worked hard but then went out at night and on the weekends, finding trouble. He also loved to fight, and his six-foot-tall, redheaded figure was known for never backing down once a fight began. His mother spent many long hours praying for her son, asking God to protect him and save him.

One night, when Alvin came home after hours of drinking and fighting, he found his mother rocking in her chair by the fire. She said, "Alvin, when are you going to be a man like your father and your grandfather?" These men were known for their honesty and love. Suddenly, Alvin looked back on his life and saw how empty and hopeless it was.

He later said, "God just took ahold of my life. My little, old mother had been praying for me for so long, and I guess the Lord finally decided to answer her."

Alvin knelt down, put his head in his mother's lap, and the two of them cried together as he gave his life to God. He promised his mother that he would leave his drinking, gambling, and fighting behind. "I will live the life God wants me to live," he said.

And that's what he did. He became an elder in his church and led the singing on Sundays, and he took his faith seriously. So seriously, in fact, that he almost didn't go when his country called upon him to fight in the First World War.

In June 1917, Alvin received a postcard in the mail that told him he would need to join the army and train as a soldier. The problem was, Alvin believed that the sixth commandment ("Do not murder") meant he couldn't fight in a war. He believed war was wrong. Alvin wanted to stay home in Tennessee; get married to Gracie, the woman he loved; and work his farm.

When he talked to his pastor about the war, Alvin said, "I've been converted to the gospel of peace and love and of 'Do good for evil.' Fight! Kill! I never killed nobody, even in my bad days, and I don't want to begin now."

Remembering his promise to his mother that he would never fight again, Alvin was stuck. He wanted to be a good American citizen and help his country, but he didn't want to hurt anyone, and he especially couldn't imagine killing another human. He asked the army for an exemption so that he wouldn't have to fight. But the army denied his request and sent him to training in Georgia.

The trip to Georgia was Alvin's first time outside his county, first time on a train, first time for many things. Soon, he found himself in New York City, sailing past the Statue of Liberty on his way to Europe to fight against Germany. He was nervous about fighting, but he had spent many long hours studying his Bible and praying for guidance. He knew he was doing what he needed to do. He didn't understand why or what God's plan was, but he knew he was supposed to go.

The American soldiers joined up with their friends and allies in France to fight off the Germans. In September 1918, the battle for the Argonne Forest began. German troops depended on the railroad lines to get their supplies, and the Allied forces planned to cut off those supplies so the Germans would be forced to surrender. As the soldiers marched closer to the Germans, they walked through dense trees, barbed wire, and the fire of German machine guns.

Alvin's company stayed still during the day and walked by night, but that didn't keep them from being seen and shot at. Alvin watched as friends and enemies fell dead, and he prayed for both Germans and Americans as he walked. The Germans attacked with poison gas, but the Americans still walked on, struggling to get their gas masks on as they slogged through the rain and fog.

On October 8, Alvin and his fellow soldiers were crawling forward under tree trunks and bushes, hiding from the machine guns that shot all around. Alvin and sixteen other men were sent around the left side of the battle, into German territory. They stopped, trying to decide what to do next and where to attack, when suddenly, two German stretcher bearers appeared, carrying an empty stretcher. They saw the Americans and instantly dropped their stretcher and ran into the woods. The Americans chased them, afraid they would alert other soldiers, who would then come and shoot at them. Running through the trees, the Americans came upon twenty or thirty German soldiers sitting around, eating breakfast, unarmed.

The Germans dropped their dishes, held up their hands, and surrendered to the Americans. But suddenly, German machine guns in the distance turned and began firing on Alvin and his fellow soldiers. Within a few seconds, six Americans had been killed, and three were wounded. Of the eight soldiers left, Alvin was the highest ranking, so he took command of his soldiers and the twenty or more prisoners, all of whom were flat on the ground, hiding from the gunfire behind trees and stumps.

But Alvin wasn't hiding, he was firing back. Every time a German soldier stood up to fire on the Americans, Alvin would fire. But he didn't want to kill anyone. "I kept yelling at them to come down," he said. "I didn't want to kill any more than I had to. But it was they or I."

A German lieutenant decided to attack Alvin with a group of six men who had bayonets fixed to their guns. As they headed toward him in a single file line, Alvin remembered a hunting trick from back home. When ducks were flying in a line, if he shot the leader, the others would scatter in fear. But if he shot the one in the back, the others wouldn't notice and would keep flying as he worked his way forward. So, instead of firing

7

at the first man coming at him, he fired at the last one, then the next-to-last, and so on. When he finally fired on the first man, he was almost within reach. If Alvin had missed even once, he would have been dead.

When he turned around to gather the soldiers and prisoners, he discovered the German commander was holding a pistol. When Alvin grabbed it, he realized it was hot. While Alvin was taking out the machine guns and bayonets, he was being shot at from behind, but without injury. God had protected him.

Alvin ordered the men to stand up, and he began to lead them to the American lines. As they walked, they came upon more groups of German soldiers. But these soldiers assumed they were being captured by a large company of Americans, so they immediately surrendered. They continued to gather more and more prisoners, and Alvin was grateful not to shoot his gun many more times.

Three hours after Alvin and his company set out on their mission, he came to the American lines, leading seven fellow American soldiers and 132 German prisoners.

Later that night, Alvin wrote a few lines about what had happened that day, then wrote this:

> So you can see here in this case of mine where God helped me out. I had [been] living for God and working the church some time before I come to the army. So I am a witness to the fact that God did help me out of that hard battle; for the bushes were shot up all around me and I never got a scratch.

In the days that followed, Alvin learned which of his friends and fellow soldiers had been killed, and he helped bury them where they fell. He also retraced his steps for commanders who wanted to know the details of what had happened. Because of his bravery and skill, he was promoted from corporal to sergeant. He wrote a postcard home to his family, but didn't write anything about his bravery or the prisoners he had captured. He didn't think much of it.

But other people certainly thought what he had done was amazing. He received awards and medals, and General John J. Pershing, commander of the American forces, called Alvin "the greatest civilian soldier of the war." The French commander told him, "What you did was the greatest thing accomplished by any private soldier of all the armies of Europe."

Shortly after that event, the war ended. Alvin was ordered to visit American soldiers around France, sharing his story and encouraging the men as they waited to return home. He enjoyed the opportunity to travel and especially to talk about his faith in God, who had protected and comforted him. On April 8, Alvin went to the Palace of Versailles to witness the signing of the peace treaty that ended World War I.

Because of what he had done, he was called a hero and given many honors. But Alvin didn't like reliving the events of that morning in October. He didn't want to be a hero for killing people, even though he did what he had to do to save the lives of many others. Now that the war was over, he was ready to be home with his mother and the woman he loved, Gracie Williams. When he climbed aboard the ship bound for New York City, he was thrilled to be going home.

When he arrived, though, he was greeted by reporters and thousands of people cheering his name. Word about the hero Alvin York had spread across the ocean to America, and the people wanted to get a glimpse of him. As he traveled to his hotel in New York, crowds lined the streets, cheering and throwing streamers. He was offered many thousands of dollars (probably over $3 million in today's economy) to turn his story into a movie and let his name and picture be used in advertisements. He turned it all down, only wanting to get back home to Tennessee.

Finally, after meeting famous, wealthy people and politicians, he boarded a train bound for

Tennessee. He greeted his family and started making plans to marry Gracie. Their wedding was performed by the governor of Tennessee and attended by more than 2,500 people. Alvin was still getting offers for lots of money, but he was ready to settle down and work his farm.

Over time, Alvin realized he might be able to do something good with the money he was being offered. He had never been able to go to school for long, and he wanted other children in his town to gain the knowledge he didn't have. So, he decided to build a school—the York Institute—for kids in his community to receive a good education. Later, he also built a Bible school. When a movie was made about him in 1941, he used his share of the money for his school. When he traveled around, speaking throughout America, he used the money he earned to help his community. When he was making plans for his school, he wrote:

> Since I came home I have been offered a
> thousand dollars a day, but I remembered

those lines in the little book that I always carry with me. "What shall a man profit if he gain the whole world and lose his own soul?" And I felt that if I accepted that offer, that if I forgot those boys and girls in Fentress County, I would be losing my own soul. So instead, I'm giving my time to help them. I'd rather see them totter to and from a good school every day than to have half a million dollars in the bank.

For the rest of his life, this is what Alvin did. He lived simply and devoted himself to serving and helping others—raising money for the school, feeding whomever happened to be around at mealtimes, getting jobs for people in need, leading the singing in his church, and faithfully loving his wife. He was a normal man who knew God had given him much so that he could use it to serve those around him.

SOURCE

John Perry, *Sgt. York: His Life, Legend, and Legacy* (Nashville: Broadman & Holman, 1997).

Strength in Generosity

Most people think of Sergeant York as a hero for his bravery on the battlefield, but his truly heroic act was living a generous life. He didn't use his fame to make himself rich but to help others and point them to God.

Generosity isn't always an easy way to live. Our world tells us success looks like having the nicest stuff, going on amazing vacations, and wearing the best clothes. But what if we thought more like Alvin York? What if success is really living a generous life—serving and giving things to other people—instead of just looking out for ourselves?

This is what Jesus taught in His Sermon on the Mount, which was one of Alvin's favorite Bible passages. Jesus said that where our treasure is, that's where our hearts will be also. Basically, we will love our treasure more than anything else. So, if stuff is our treasure, that's what we will love, think about, and spend our time on.

But Alvin knew there was much more to life than stuff. Jesus was his true treasure, and He can be yours as well.

Have you ever prayed that Jesus would be your treasure—what you love more than anything else? Ask Him to change your heart to love Him more. That's a prayer He loves to answer.

Questions

1. How did Alvin York's life change after he became a Christian?

2. How was his faith in God reflected in the way he fought in the war?

3. When he wrote to his family after the battle in which he captured 132 men, he didn't mention what he had done. What does this tell you about him?

4. After the war, Alvin was offered large amounts of money to be in advertisements and to write articles.

Everyone wanted his name on their products, but he refused. Do you think that was an easy choice for him? Why, or why not? What would you do?

5. Read Matthew 6:19–21. What does it mean to "store up treasures in heaven"? How did Alvin do this? How can you do it?

"For where your TREASURE is, there your HEART will be also."–Matthew 6:21

"Moment by moment, I DEPEND ON HIM.
If I were left to MYSELF,
my faith would utterly FAIL."

George Müller

FAITH

When he was a boy, no one could have predicted that George Müller would grow up to love Jesus and take care of more than ten thousand children. Born on September 27, 1805, in the kingdom of Prussia (now part of Germany), George spent his childhood getting into trouble with his brother; by the time he was ten years old, he had stolen tax money from his father, an accountant, several times. When he was fourteen, his mother died. Rather than changing his life and giving up his sinful activities, he spent that night gambling until early in the morning. He continued to steal, lie, and live a sinful life. After stealing from an innkeeper when he was sixteen, George was arrested and sent to prison, where he stayed for a year. When he got out, he went back to his old ways.

On the outside, he looked like someone who was working hard at school. He knew six languages—Latin, Greek, Hebrew, German, French, and English. Teachers and students liked him, but he was living only for himself. When he felt bad about his sin, he would decide to change his ways. But a few days or weeks later, he would be back to doing the same things all over again.

When he was twenty, George and three friends decided to travel to Switzerland, where he had always wanted to go. But on the trip, he secretly cheated his friends—George kept track of the money, and he would lie and tell his friends things cost more than they did so he wouldn't have to pay as much as his friends paid. After the trip, he felt sad. Even though he had gone where he dreamed of going, he wasn't happy.

But God hadn't given up on him.

One day, George took a walk with a friend named Beta, who had gone on the trip to Switzerland with him. Beta went to a prayer meeting at a Christian's house every Saturday. The group that gathered would sing, pray, and read a sermon. George was curious and went with Beta to the meeting that evening. He had never heard anyone pray the way these people prayed. On their way home, George told Beta, "Everything we have seen on our journey to Switzerland and all of our former pleasures are nothing in comparison with this evening."

George went back to the Christian's house the next day and for several days after. Together, they read the Bible and prayed. God was working in George's heart. Even though other students laughed at him, George began to talk about Jesus and being a Christian. When he wrote to his father and brother to tell them about his new faith in Christ, he encouraged them to seek the Lord, telling them how happy he now was. Having found what was truly important in life, he thought they would want the same happiness. Instead, they responded with an angry letter. His father disowned him, saying he would no longer consider George as his son.

Continuing to grow in his faith, George began to train as a pastor and preach in churches. His sermons were on Bible passages that talked about sin and our need for a Savior. Some people didn't like his style of preaching—they were used to hearing things that made them feel better about themselves, not messages calling on them to admit their sin and repent. But even though some people rejected him, others trusted Jesus after hearing George preach. He began to learn the importance of letting God guide him as he studied and preached. He wrote in his journal: "I am glad that I learned the importance of ministering in God's power alone. I can do all things through Christ, but without Him, I can accomplish nothing."

One day, George received a letter from a pastor in Bristol, England, asking him to come and join the work in that town. George and his wife prayed and saw that was where God wanted them, so they moved to Bristol, England. While living and preaching there, George discovered that many of the people in the town were very poor. He said to himself, "If only the Lord would give me the means to help them!" An hour later, someone gave him sixty pounds (close to $7,000 in today's economy), which he used to buy bread for the poor.

God was teaching George the importance of depending and waiting on Him for everything. During that time, it was normal for pastors to be paid by renting out the pews (benches) in the church. Each family would pay a certain amount monthly for their pew—the best seats going to those who paid the most. George saw that this was unfair to the poor, who couldn't pay for their seats and, therefore, had to sit or stand in the back. He knew this was against the teaching of the New Testament. So, he said he would not rent out pews or collect a normal salary. Instead, a box was placed in the church where people could give money as God led them to. This meant George and his wife never knew when they would receive money. But they knew God would provide, and they prayed that He would meet their daily needs. Knowing Jesus taught that we are not to store up treasure on earth, they relied on Him to give them all they needed, but they gave up any desire to have lots of earthly possessions. Just as God helped him in his preaching and teaching, He helped him with his daily food, clothing, and other needs.

George and his pastor friend opened schools to teach both children and adults about God. But one day, they heard about a boy who was an orphan and had gone to one of their day schools for a while until he was taken to a poorhouse (a place for people with no home) outside the city. This boy was so sad that he could no longer attend the school. When George heard this, he began to think of how he might help poor children in Bristol who needed a place to live.

He continued to think and pray about this, finally deciding he should open an orphan house, where children would be cared for. Most people who came up with an idea like that would then put together a business plan and talk to wealthy people, asking them for money. But George thought the orphan house was a perfect opportunity to show the people in Bristol that God is faithful. He wanted to show that we can rely on God—that He is the One who meets our needs.

So, George decided he would never ask anyone for money for the orphan house. He would simply pray about it and trust God to provide. When a need came up—for money to rent a house, for clothing, food, and furniture—George prayed about it. He asked God to put it in people's hearts to send what was needed. And then he watched and waited for God to answer. The answer didn't always come right away; many times, they had to wait days and even weeks to see prayers answered. But God provided everything the orphans needed.

One day, the children were led into the dining room to eat breakfast, but there was no food at all in the house. There were dishes and silverware, but nothing to eat. George told the children to sit, and he led them in prayer, thanking God for the food they were going to have. Suddenly, there was a knock on the door. The baker had come with a basket full of bread. He explained that God had caused him to wake in the night and put it on his heart to go and bake bread for the children at the orphan house. So, he did.

As the baker was leaving, the milkman appeared at the door. He was taking a load of milk in his cart when a wheel came off right in front of the orphan house. He needed help fixing it, but he was afraid the milk would be stolen if he left it sitting there and offered the milk to the orphans instead.

In a matter of minutes, the children had their breakfast along with fresh proof that God provides everything we need—we need only to ask and trust Him.

Over and over, George experienced miraculous answers to his prayers. Sometimes people gave pennies; other times, huge amounts of money. In every case, he learned to thank God for providing just what they needed, no matter the amount.

Some people tried to convince him to tell others what was needed. They thought people would give when the idea of the orphan house was new and exciting, but if George didn't tell them about the needs later, they would forget and not give anymore.

George knew that God can do anything He pleases, including putting it in people's minds and hearts to give money, food, clothing—whatever is needed at any given moment.

One day, he wrote in his journal:

> The Lord has again given us this day our daily bread, although in the morning there was not the least prospect of obtaining supplies. We are trusting in God day by day. He meets our needs faithfully in so many ways as we wait patiently upon Him. Our needs are great, but His help is also great.

George didn't want people to think God would answer prayers only about churches and orphan houses or that He would answer only the prayers that special people prayed. Instead, he wrote his autobiography, telling these stories of God's provision, because he wanted every Christian to realize that he or she had the same access to God and could experience the same kind of miracles. God loves to answer the prayers of His children.

He also wanted people to realize that giving to others for the sake of the gospel is far better than buying things that we want. When we give to others so that they might know about Jesus—by supporting missionaries and churches and ministries like the orphan house—we're doing what Jesus talked about: storing up treasures in heaven. When we do this, we remember that God's kingdom is what is most important.

In the end, George Müller's orphan ministry grew to the point that they had to buy land and build more orphan homes. More than ten thousand children were cared for in the Bristol Orphan Homes during his lifetime, and the Müllers' organization continues to care for children and the poor today. Many children who came through the orphanage became Christians, going out from there to share the good news about Jesus with others. God provided over a million British pounds for the expenses throughout George's life, which would be more than $100 million in today's money. And George never had to ask for a penny of it.

But George never claimed to be special for having such strong faith. He knew it was a gift from God: "I give the glory to God alone that He has enabled me to trust in Him, and He has not permitted my confidence in Him to fail."

SOURCES

George Müller, *The Autobiography of George Müller* (New Kensington, PA: Whitaker House, 1985).

Mullers.org.

Strength in Faith

Do you think you could have the kind of faith George had? Sometimes faith can feel hard. It would have been easier for him just to ask people for what he needed. People probably would have helped him. But who would have received the fame and glory for that? Not God, but George.

It's easy to hear a story like this and think, *Wow, George Müller had amazing faith in God.* But from his own words, we know that's not what he ever wanted people to think. He wrote, "My faith is the same faith which is found in every believer." Any faith he had was given to him by God. George's story was never about George, but about God's plan to show how faithful and strong He is so that other people might know and trust Him.

That's His plan for you too. You may never build homes to care for thousands of orphans, but you have opportunities to trust God right where you are. Maybe that means trusting God to give you what you truly need and to help you serve others, even if He doesn't give you the new video game, shoes, bike, or other fun thing you want. Maybe it means trusting Him to make you happy in *Him* instead of in things you own or do.

Before he trusted Christ, George lived his life running around chasing happiness, but he was never satisfied. Then he realized he could be truly happy only when his soul was happy in the Lord. So, he lived simply the rest of his days—not owning stuff or traveling to amazing places. He didn't have to worry about losing things because he trusted that God would care for all his needs. And God did.

And He will for you too.

Questions

---

1. In Mark 9, a father brings his son to Jesus, desperate for Jesus to heal him. Jesus says, "Everything is possible for the one who believes" (v. 23). How does the father respond in verse 24?

2. What do you think the father's words mean? Can he believe and also not believe at the same time?

3. How does this encourage you if you ever struggle to have faith in God? Have you ever asked Him to give you that faith?

4. Even with all the things George Müller did in his life, his first goal was for his soul to be happy in the Lord. He wrote, "The primary business I must attend to every day is to fellowship with the Lord." What do you think it means to fellowship with the Lord? (Hint: Other words for *fellowship* are *companionship* and *friendship*.)

5. Read Philippians 4:6. What does Paul say we should do when we're worried about something?

6. Are you worried about anything today? Take a minute to pray and trust God with it, asking Him for faith to trust that He will take care of it.

Those who know your name **TRUST** in you because you have not abandoned those who seek you, LORD. —Psalm 9:10

"Do not desire to be STRONG, POWERFUL, HONORED and RESPECTED, but let GOD ALONE be your STRENGTH, your FAME and your HONOR."

Dietrich Bonhoeffer
COURAGE

Dietrich Bonhoeffer and his twin sister, Sabine, were born on February 4, 1906. They were the sixth and seventh out of eight children in their family and were close throughout their lives.

As a boy, Dietrich loved to play chess, cards, and guessing games. He and his siblings would dig caves and build tents in their garden, and they loved pets, keeping at different times lizards, snakes, squirrels, pigeons, and an assortment of beetles and butterflies. In school, he was a jumper and sprinter, and he loved reading and music.

When he was still young, he decided he wanted to be a pastor and study theology (the study of God). He was interested in the church and the Bible, but he would later realize he didn't truly have a relationship with God.

During the First World War, Dietrich's older brother Walter was killed as a soldier. Dietrich was too young to fight, but he felt the effects of the conflict in his family and his country. When

Germany lost the war, the winning countries imposed large fines on Germany. Because the country had to pay so much money, the German people suffered greatly, and many were starving. Dietrich's family was affected by these conditions, but he was still able to continue his education to become a pastor.

In school, Dietrich gained a reputation as someone who thought for himself. He didn't believe everything he was told or go along with the crowd; instead, he listened and thought through things, trying to find the truth. Then, he stood up for what he believed. This would become a very important trait later in his life.

During his training as a pastor, one of his roles was teaching kids. Dietrich loved children, and when his nieces and nephews did their homework in the garden next to his home, he would throw chocolates out his window to them. He loved to tell Bible stories in an exciting way, showing the children that God's Word is living and active. He spent a lot of his time training young boys and men in their faith, especially those who wanted to be pastors.

Because of the suffering the German people endured after World War I, many were angry and humiliated, looking for a way to raise their nation back up as a world power. When a new leader, Adolf Hitler, began his rise to power, he said things many people liked. He talked about the German people being powerful and having pride in their country. He wanted to help Germany get back their power and status in the world, and he built a group of soldiers and officers called Nazis to do so. Only, Hitler had sinful ideas about who could be considered true Germans. Eventually, his plans for Germany's victory would include the suffering and murder of millions of people.

Many pastors and church leaders liked what Hitler was saying. They saw that he had great power, and they wanted to get close to him so the church could have power and influence too. Dietrich saw that these leaders were not interested in following Christ or truly teaching the

Bible; they were interested in their own glory, not God's.

It was easy to go to church and call yourself a Christian without really following Jesus. Many people, even pastors, were doing that. Dietrich had also been like that, until something changed. He wrote a letter to a friend, saying:

> For the first time I discovered the Bible.
> . . . I had often preached, I had seen a great deal of the Church, and talked and preached about it—but I had not yet become a Christian. . . . Also I had never prayed, or prayed only very little.
> . . . It became clear to me that the life of a servant of Jesus Christ must belong to the Church, and step by step it became plainer to me how far that must go.

With this new faith in Christ, Dietrich was prepared to suffer and stand up for the truth, whatever might happen. When people began to hang Nazi flags at the front of churches, he preached against it. When friends who were pastors began to follow Hitler's orders to persecute Jews, he told them he could no longer work or be friends with them.

He knew his students would also face persecution and suffering, so he told them in a sermon: "Do not desire to be strong, powerful, honored and respected, but let God alone be your strength, your fame and your honor."

Dietrich depended on God for strength over and over during Germany's time under Hitler. But he didn't do so perfectly. When his brother-in-law's Jewish father died, Dietrich was asked to preach the funeral message. But he was told by church leaders that he shouldn't do a funeral service for someone who was Jewish, so he didn't. He let fear of what other people would say keep him from helping his family. Later, he wrote to his brother-in-law that he was sorry for his fear, saying, "It's the kind of thing one can never make up for. So all I can do is to ask you to forgive my weakness then. I know now for certain that I ought to have behaved differently."

After that, Dietrich found himself standing alone at times; he was firmly against excluding Jewish Christians—people from Jewish families who followed the teaching of Jesus Christ—from becoming pastors, but many leaders in churches went along with the Nazis' hatred of Jews and wouldn't allow them to be church leaders. Dietrich also found himself alone in his stand against pastors swearing oaths to Hitler. He took things seriously and saw a coming war. Many people thought he was crazy. Later, a British pastor friend, George Bell, wrote about Dietrich: "He was crystal clear in his convictions; and young as he was, and humble-minded as he was, he saw the truth, and spoke it with a complete absence of fear."

Perhaps because he had let fear control him before, he knew the only way to stand for truth was to do what he had preached to his students: "Let God alone be your strength."

In 1939, Dietrich left Germany for America. He was fearful of having to fight for Germany in the war, and he had been forced to end his job as a pastor because he did not go along with the Nazi ideas. In America, he was safe from danger and free to preach and write. But it wasn't long before he began to feel he had made the wrong decision in leaving Germany. He wrote to a friend, "I have made a mistake in coming to America. I must live through this difficult period of our national history with the Christian people of Germany."

So, Dietrich returned to the danger and confusion of the German capital city, Berlin. He joined a group of people who saw the danger of Hitler and wanted to do what they could to stop further damage. Hitler was pushing his military into Western countries, causing death and destruction, while also further persecuting, and, in the end, murdering, millions of people he did not consider worthy of the German name.

Realizing the horror of what Germany's leaders were doing, Dietrich became a "traitor" to his country. He began to help with plans to overthrow Hitler and impose a new government. Seeing this as his only option, Dietrich didn't believe his actions were treason but instead that they were the most patriotic things he could do. To be a German patriot, he needed to help rescue the German people from the terrifying situation they were in. For Dietrich to go along with Hitler's plans would have been the real treason against his country.

Instead, Dietrich became a double agent. He took a position in the government that would give him information and the opportunities he needed to work against Hitler and help those who were persecuted. He and other members of the resistance movement worked to remove Hitler from power and bring peace to Germany. Dietrich's own work was mostly in helping Jews who needed to get out of the country before they would be sent away to concentration camps, where they would most likely be killed.

Over time, the resistance group realized it would be impossible to remove Hitler without killing him. Deciding to be part of the plans to assassinate someone would have been unthinkable to Dietrich before now. But these were different times, and through the concentration camps and the war, Hitler was killing millions of people. Something had to be done.

Dietrich wasn't the one to build bombs or place them where they might kill Hitler. He was involved in the background, helping with plans and connections. But he waited in anticipation when a bomb was placed on Hitler's airplane. The bomb failed to explode. Then another plan was hatched in which a military officer waited as Hitler toured a military arsenal, looking for a chance to get close enough to him to set off a bomb. But rather than staying for the expected thirty minutes, Hitler was there only ten minutes, which wasn't enough time.

Many people didn't know what Dietrich was doing. From the outside, it looked like he was changing his mind and now working for Hitler and the Nazis. We know now he was secretly working tirelessly to bring an end to the horror of Hitler's rule, but to many who knew him, Dietrich looked like someone who was working with the Nazis.

Dietrich decided it was worth being embarrassed and humiliated if he could make the future better for those who would come after him. He gave up his good reputation with some in the church and in theological studies. He gave up being well-liked and respected and, instead, embraced being misunderstood and condemned.

And he paid for it. Greatly.

On April 5, 1943, Dietrich was arrested and charged with "subversion of the armed forces," which meant he was accused of working against Germany's military. He spent the next eighteen months in a prison in Berlin, where he worked hard to stand up to the interrogators who questioned him about what he had done. He also wanted to be careful not to make things worse for his coconspirators, who had also been arrested. They worked out a way to knock on the walls to communicate and also hid letters in books and laundry bags.

Some of the other resistance workers were in different prisons, so they developed a code system to give each other information. A family member would bring Dietrich a book, and then, starting from the back of the book, he would make a light pencil line under one letter every ten pages. His family would then work for hours to find the pencil marks, put the messages together, and deliver them to other prisoners.

For more than a year, Dietrich held out hope that he would be released. But as more evidence against him turned up, the family began planning his escape. The plan was for him to put on a mechanic's uniform that the family was able to secretly get to him, and then a friendly guard had agreed to help him escape.

But a few days later, Dietrich's older brother was arrested, so Dietrich gave up the escape plan so that it wouldn't make things worse for his brother and other family members.

He was moved to another prison. Then, as the end of the war drew closer, he was moved again, this time to an air-raid shelter in a concentration camp. He stayed there seven weeks before being moved one last time to a place called Flossenbürg in a journey that took seven days. Once he left Berlin, his family didn't know where he was, and their letters to him were returned. They tried repeatedly to find him, but couldn't.

The Sunday after Easter, in the prison at Flossenbürg, Dietrich preached a small church service for the other prisoners in his cell. He read 1 Peter 1:3: "Blessed be the God and Father of our Lord Jesus Christ. Because of his great mercy he has given us new birth into a living hope through the resurrection of Jesus Christ from the dead." He talked about their captivity and how healing comes through Jesus. When he finished, the prisoners in another cell wanted to smuggle him over to their room so he could preach a service there also.

Suddenly, the door opened, and he heard a voice call out, "Prisoner Bonhoeffer, get ready and come with us!"

He quickly gathered his things so they could be given to his family and said these words to his British friend and fellow prisoner, Payne Best: "This is the end—for me the beginning of life."

The camp doctor later wrote about seeing Dietrich in his final moments:

> Through the half-open door in one room of the huts I saw Pastor Bonhoeffer, before taking off his prison garb, kneeling on the floor praying fervently to his God. I was most deeply moved by the way this lovable man prayed, so devout and so certain that God heard his prayer. At the place of execution, he again said a short prayer and then climbed the steps to the gallows, brave and composed. His death ensued after a few seconds. In the almost fifty years that I worked as a doctor, I have hardly ever seen a man die so entirely submissive to the will of God.

Dietrich Bonhoeffer was killed on April 9, 1945. Two weeks later, the Allied forces fighting against Germany came in and freed the people held at the concentration camp at Flossenbürg.

Later, his friend Payne Best wrote about Dietrich, "He had always been afraid that he would not be strong enough to stand such a test, but now he knew there was nothing in life of which one need ever be afraid."

SOURCE

Eberhard Bethge, *Dietrich Bonhoeffer: Man of Vision, Man of Courage* (New York: Harper & Row, 1970).

Strength in Courage

You probably won't be called on to die for what you believe. But you will have opportunities to be courageous. It could be something public—like standing up against someone who is bullying another kid. Or it could be private—choosing not to look at or watch things you know you shouldn't.

Before he had to make serious choices about standing up or giving up, Dietrich Bonhoeffer already knew he couldn't rely on his own strength. He knew he was weak. But he knew God would be his strength when he was weak and his honor when he was shamed and embarrassed.

We've all seen movies or shows where someone stands up to a bully, and then the bully stops picking on people or even becomes their friend. It's a little easier to consider standing up for what's right when we think things might turn out that way. But they didn't for Dietrich. Sure, Hitler soon lost the war. But not before Dietrich lost his life. Yet Dietrich knew his real life was already "hidden with Christ in God" (Colossians 3:3), and he had nothing to fear. You can know the same thing—if your life is in Christ, you have nothing to fear.

Questions

1. Read Hebrews 13:6. How does this verse apply to Dietrich's story? What did man do to him? Why should we not fear?

2. Do you fear taking a stand? Do you worry what other people will think?

3. Like Dietrich Bonhoeffer, Paul was also put to death by government leaders. What kind of rescue do you think Paul was writing about in 2 Timothy 4:18? Was he wrong when he wrote this verse, or could he have been talking about a different kind of rescue and safety? (Hint: The end of the verse tells us what safety is.)

4. What are some of your fears? Spend some time praying that God will be your strength and help you be courageous, even when it's embarrassing or scary.

The Lord is my HELPER; I will not be AFRAID. What can MAN do to me?—Hebrews 13:6

"The real calling is not a certain **PLACE** or **CAREER** but to **EVERYDAY OBEDIENCE**. And that call is extended to **EVERY** CHRISTIAN, not just a select few."

Brother Andrew
OBEDIENCE

Born May 11, 1928, in Holland, Andrew was one of six children in his family. Each Sunday, the family walked to church together. Andrew, though, had a habit of sitting in the back of the church and sneaking out to skate on frozen canals or sit in fields. He would then rush back to the church building and listen carefully to the conversations as people left, picking up just enough about the service to later fake that he had been there. He didn't want to get in trouble, but he had no interest in hearing about God.

The day before Andrew's twelfth birthday, World War II reached his world as the first German planes flew over his small village. Germany bombed parts of Holland, and Holland, unable to defend itself, quickly surrendered. For the next five years, German soldiers occupied Andrew's village. The people had little to eat and suffered greatly. The school was closed when Andrew was in the sixth grade, so he never received a full education. But while others were suffering, Andrew spent the first part of the German occupation playing pranks on the soldiers—exploding cherry bombs and firecrackers near the Germans and making them chase him. He had a thirst for adventure and ran all over his little town looking for it.

When he was seventeen, Andrew joined the army, still looking for adventure. He was sent to Indonesia, where Holland was fighting to hold on to control of the Dutch East Indies. Before he went, his mother held out her Bible to him and asked if he would take it. He agreed, and she asked if he would read it. Again, he said yes, but buried it deep in his bag and forgot it.

War was not the adventure Andrew had hoped for. He was disgusted with the killing. It was one thing to shoot at paper targets but something else when the targets were human beings. He wanted to forget the things he had seen, so he started drinking and fighting other soldiers. After being in Indonesia for more than two years, he took a bullet in his ankle and was instantly out of the war. The doctors discussed amputating his foot but decided to leave it. He was told he would never again be able to walk without a cane.

While he was recovering, Andrew noticed that the nurses caring for him were always cheerful. One day, Andrew asked why and was told it was the love of Christ that caused them to have so much joy. He started to read the Bible his mother had given him, beginning with Genesis 1:1. When he arrived home in Holland, he continued to spend hours reading the Bible and went to church and Bible studies wherever he could find them. On a stormy winter night in 1950, Andrew lay in bed and prayed, "Lord, if You will show me the way, I will follow You. Amen."

From that day on, Andrew was devoted to God and wanted to learn all he could about Him. He began to think he might be called to be a missionary, and he was advised by other Christians to begin his missions work right where he lived. So, he found a job in a factory where he was one of the few Christians, along with a young woman named Corrie. The two of them talked about Jesus with their fellow workers, many of whom were harsh and cruel and treated them badly. But God was working through them, and He began to change the lives of some of the factory workers, including one of the meanest women who worked there. Andrew was learning to pray and then to act in obedience as God led him.

But still he wondered whether God wanted him to continue at the factory or move on as a missionary. As he sat alone outside one day, praying, he called out to God:

> "What is it, Lord? What am I holding back? What am I using as an excuse for not serving You in whatever You want me to do?"
>
> And then, there by the canal, I finally had my answer. My "yes" to God had always been a "yes, but." Yes, but I'm not educated. Yes, but I'm lame.

With the next breath, I did say, "Yes." I said it in a brand-new way, without qualification. "I'll go, Lord," I said. . . . "Whenever, wherever, however You want me, I'll go. And I'll begin this very minute. Lord, as I stand up from this place, and as I take my first step forward, will You consider that this is a step toward complete obedience to You? I'll call it the Step of Yes."

When he stood up and took a step without his cane, Andrew felt a sharp pain in his lame leg and picked up his foot. When he put it back on the ground, he could stand on it with no pain or need for a cane. He slowly took more steps and wondered if it was possible that he had been healed. As the days went on, it became clear: God had chosen to heal him.

Deciding to pursue his goal of being a missionary, Andrew moved to Glasgow, Scotland, to attend a missionary training school. After several weeks, Andrew and his fellow students were sent out on a training trip through Scotland. Each student on his team was given a one-pound banknote (about $40 in today's economy). They were to use that money for transportation, hotels, food, renting space for gospel meetings, and anything else they might need. Not only that, but when they returned to school after four weeks, they were to pay back the one-pound notes they had received. And one more thing: they weren't allowed to ask people for money; they had to rely on God alone to provide what they needed each step of the way.

As Andrew and four other young men traveled around Scotland, God always provided. A parent would send a little money just when it was needed, or a church would send a check. People gave them food—in one small town they were given six hundred eggs! But they never told anyone they needed money, and they always quickly gave away ten percent of what they received.

As they held meetings in one city, many young people came the first day, and the team wanted to find a way to make sure they came back the next day. So, one team member got up and said, "Before the meeting tomorrow evening we'd like you all to have tea with us here. Four o'clock. How many think they can make it?"

More than twenty people raised their hands. Now the team would have to come up with tea, cake, bread and butter, and cups for all these people—with no money. After the meeting, many of the students offered to help, saying they would bring tea, cups, milk, sugar. But they had no cake, which was essential for a Scottish tea. That night, the team prayed and asked God to provide a cake.

The next day, the team waited expectantly for the cake. They received letters, but no money. The tea was scheduled for four o'clock, but with fifteen minutes left, there still was no cake. Then, they heard the doorbell. The mailman held a large box. He said it felt like food, and even though the delivery day was over, he hated to leave food sitting around until the next day. The package was addressed to Andrew from a friend in London with whom he had lived for a while. There was no note inside, but as he lifted the lid, he saw an "enormous, glistening, moist, chocolate cake."

This lesson about God's ability to provide would serve Andrew for years to come. When he was almost ready to return home from the training school, he saw a magazine with an announcement of a youth festival that would take place in Warsaw, Poland, that summer. It said everyone was invited. Andrew decided to write the people organizing the festival to ask if they would allow him, a Christian, to come. Poland was now a Communist country, and Communist leaders did not approve of Christianity. But they did, in fact, want Andrew to come.

This first trip began decades of ministry in Communist countries. Many Christians in these countries suffered greatly. They had very few Bibles, as most had been taken away. They couldn't worship freely. The government controlled many of the churches. Christians lost their jobs. Children were expelled from school for praying before meals. Andrew knew God was leading him to work in these countries. But how?

One day a friend named Karl knocked on his door and asked Andrew if he knew how to drive. This friend was from a church that had been praying faithfully for Andrew, and Karl believed God wanted Andrew to learn to drive a car. But Andrew's family didn't have a car, and he said he would certainly never own one. They were too expensive. Why should he learn to drive?

A week later, Karl returned and asked if Andrew had been taking driving lessons. Andrew said he had not. Karl said, "Haven't you learned yet how important obedience is? I suppose I'm going to have to teach you myself. Hop in."

A few weeks later, Andrew passed his driving test and received a license. But he still didn't see why he needed it. Karl said, "That's the excitement in obedience. Finding out later what God had in mind."

Time passed, and Andrew decided to try to get into Yugoslavia as a missionary. This Communist country was closed to many outsiders. But Andrew received his visa (a pass from the government) to enter the country and called a Christian friend who was like a father to him to share the good news. The friend answered, "Andrew, you'd better come home for your keys." But Andrew didn't know what he meant. The friend said he and his wife had decided months before that if Andrew received a visa to Yugoslavia, they would give him their new Volkswagen car. So, *this* was why he needed to learn to drive.

As Andrew pulled up to the guard station on the Yugoslavian border, he glanced around his car filled with Bibles and Christian literature. Printed material was often confiscated at the border because the government didn't want people bringing in what they called "foreign propaganda" that might cause the people in their country to become dissatisfied with their lives. As he looked around, Andrew prayed what he called the "Prayer of God's Smuggler":

> Lord, in my luggage I have Scripture that I want to take to Your children across this border. When You were on

earth, You made blind eyes see. Now, I
pray, make seeing eyes blind. Do not let
the guards see those things You do not
want them to see.

Indeed, again and again, guards at borders of
these Communist countries had every opportunity
to see the Bibles and other Christian writing in
Andrew's car, some of which was in plain sight, yet
God caused them not to see in miraculous ways.

On one trip to Bulgaria, Andrew attended a
small, secret church service at a home one night.
There was no singing because the people had
to be very quiet so they wouldn't be caught and
arrested. But Andrew spoke to the people, sharing with them the words of God from the Bible.
When he finished, he gave the people a Bible. All
at once, the people were so excited they almost
cried out too loudly. They all gave Andrew hugs,
then reverently passed the Bible around the room,
each one opening and closing it, feeling its pages.
These people had lived years without a Bible, and
now they had one to share.

Over time, the work continued, and God brought a few partners to join Andrew in his missions. He also brought Andrew a wife—Corrie, the young woman who had worked with him in the factory. As he entered Communist countries more frequently, he decided to go by his first name only, to protect himself and those working with him, so he was called "Brother Andrew." He also went to other Communist countries, like China and Cuba, always bringing Bibles and looking for ways to encourage Christians. After the fall of Communism in the late 1980s, Brother Andrew continued to encourage believers in former Communist countries and also expanded his ministry to the Middle East.

The work he did grew and became the organization now called Open Doors, which exists to encourage Christians in countries around the world where they are persecuted for their faith. Andrew's book, *God's Smuggler*, has sold over ten million copies and has been translated into thirty-five languages.

SOURCE
Brother Andrew with John and Elizabeth Sherrill, *God's Smuggler* (Grand Rapids, MI: Chosen Books, 2001).

Strength in Obedience

When I was told to do something as a kid, I wanted to know why I should do it. Why should I make my bed when I was just going to unmake it again at night? Why work hard in school at something I was never going to use in "real life"? If I was asked to clean up, my response was often "Why?" instead of "Okay."

Brother Andrew learned to say okay when he was told he should learn to drive a car. He didn't know why, and he didn't do it immediately. But his friend told him, "That's the excitement in obedience. Finding out later what God had in mind." Andrew learned the importance of praying for direction and stepping out in obedience to God, even when we don't understand His plans.

It's easy for us to read this and think, *Well, I would definitely obey if it was something obvious and important like that.* We're more confused, though, about what obedience looks like for us in our lives—at home, school, sports, clubs, the neighborhood, church, or wherever else we go. What does it mean to obey God in those places?

The questions that follow will help you get to some of those answers. But there are two things you should know:

- Obedience doesn't always lead to adventure and excitement. Sometimes it's very ordinary, and it's rarely easy. But it's always worth it, and it leads to true joy.

- Failing to obey doesn't mean God doesn't love you anymore. Because of God's grace through Jesus' death and resurrection, we can be forgiven when we disobey. And that's really good news because we're likely going to disobey often.

Questions

1. By traveling around the world, Brother Andrew devoted his life to encouraging Christians, many of whom didn't have Bibles and couldn't worship in church freely. Does that change the way you think about your own freedom to worship and study your Bible? If so, how?

2. Brother Andrew said every Christian is called to "everyday obedience." What does that mean? What did that mean for Brother Andrew?

3. Read John 14:15–17. What does Jesus say we will do if we love Him? Whom does Jesus say the Father will send to help us obey?

4. What are God's commands? Look up the following verses and see what you can discover:

- 2 John 1:6
- Matthew 22:37–40

5. What is one way you can obey God this week by loving Him and loving others? Pray now that the Holy Spirit will help you obey.

Isn't it good to know God will forgive you when you don't obey? Here's a sample prayer to pray:

> *Father, I'm so sorry I disobeyed You by _____. Please forgive me. Thank You for sending Jesus to live and die for me so that I don't have to be punished for my sin. Thank You for Your forgiveness. Help me to obey You. I love You. Amen.*

God doesn't want us to live life feeling guilty— He wants us to have the joy of forgiveness. So rejoice now, knowing you've been forgiven!

"If you LOVE me, you will KEEP my commands."
–John 14:15

"Make me one to be **STRONG**,
one who will **OBEY YOU**, not people,
whatever they may ask me to do."

Elka of the Wai Wai
STANDING ALONE

In the northern part of South America, in the jungle where the countries of Guyana and Brazil meet, lives a group of native South Americans called the Wai Wai (pronounced "why why"). This is the story of one of their leaders, a man named Elka. Elka lived his days as a young boy learning to fish and hunt. His family lived in a large hut with the rest of their tribe, and the people all lived, ate, played, and worked together.

By the time Elka was fifteen, his parents had both died, and he went to live in a new village with a relative. It was time for his introduction to manhood. Entering manhood required him to take belts with many holes in them and fill the holes with large stinging ants. He then had to tie the belts to his legs, allowing the ants to sting him repeatedly. The people believed that the longer he could stand the pain, the stronger and more handsome he would become. Elka took the pain as long as he could before tears filled his eyes, and he cried out.

Now that he was a man, Elka learned how to string and shoot a bow, chop trees with an ax, and study animal droppings to discern what kinds of birds and monkeys were in the trees above. He learned the jungle calls of the tapir, toucan, and bush turkey. Along with other men, he hunted spider monkeys, shot piranhas, killed caiman alligators, and fished for the large fish in the river by his village.

The Wai Wai people lived in fear of a being called by Kworokyam (pronounced "Kwor-O-kee-um"), the center of Wai Wai religion. He could be bad or good, and he used Wai Wai men called witch doctors to do his work. These witch doctors were called to a village whenever someone was sick. They would work through the night, blowing smoke on the sick person and using special stones and charms to plead with Kworokyam for healing.

Fear of spirits was strong in the Wai Wai people. They were afraid to upset one another because they worried that someone would get revenge through the spirits that lived in different animals. There were stories of people calling on the spirits in jaguars and anacondas to attack those who had offended them. Because of the power of Kworokyam, the people were constantly making sure to do things just right so that they didn't risk upsetting the spirits.

Elka knew two main witch doctors—Mafolio and Muyuwa. Mafolio was a kind man who used his knowledge and power largely for good, but Muyuwa used his powers for evil and selfishness. One day, Elka stood outside Mafolio's hut and listened to the songs he sang as he blew on a sick person. Elka began to sing those songs as he walked through the jungle. He felt a pull inside himself toward the work and life of the witch doctors.

One night as he slept, Kworokyam revealed himself to Elka in a dream, appearing and speaking to him as a wild pig. The old granny in the village prophesied that Elka would be a witch doctor, but Elka was afraid that Kworokyam would make him evil like Muyuwa. Mafolio told Elka he should be a witch doctor who used his power for good, not evil.

The wild pig appeared to Elka again in a dream, telling him that as a witch doctor, he could not eat the meat of pigs, except for a tiny piece on the back. The pig said in the dream, "If you eat more of me than this, I will eat your spirit. If you neglect me, you will also die."

As he began learning to be a witch doctor, Elka felt more fear. He was afraid of the jungle because of the spirits that lived there. He feared his friends—that they might turn on him and call on spirits to hurt him. Looking around the village, he knew he lived in badness. The people were bad; he was bad. They murdered, stole, lied, and hurt each other. But he didn't know what to do about it. He became obsessed with the fear of death and what happened to people after they died.

One day in 1948, white men came to the village. The people were afraid, calling them "white killers." The men brought gifts and tried to talk with the Wai Wai, but they couldn't understand each other's language. The men were Neill Hawkins and his brother Bob, missionaries from America. These names were difficult in the Wai Wai language, so they called Neill "Mistokin," (which sounded like "Mistah Hawkin" in their language), and Bob they called "Bahm."

Many of the Wai Wai distrusted Mistokin and Bahm. The missionaries studied the Wai Wai language, slowly learning to talk a bit. One day, Elka saw Bahm take a sharp, shiny object from a box and stick it into a sick man's arm. In a few days, the man was well. When Elka got sick, Bahm gave him medicine. Elka had planned to use his charms and blow on himself, but he trusted Bahm and took the medicine. Bahm told Elka that if the pills didn't work, he would stick him (give him a shot) the next day. The next day, Elka was well. He was thankful for the medicine, but promised himself he would never let Bahm stick him. He would rather die first.

One day, Mistokin gathered the Wai Wai people together. He had learned enough of their language to tell them God had made them and there were two ways in the world—one that led toward God and one that led away from Him.

Elka sat in his hammock, thinking about these words. *Who was this God?* The people discussed and tried to understand what Mistokin had said. They talked about Jesus, who Mistokin had said was God's Son. They saw that the love of Jesus to die for people was very different from the Wai Wai love. They loved for what they could get from others, but not to give. Yet many still feared the white men and were thankful when they left the village for a while.

Shortly after Mistokin and Bahm left, sickness spread through the village. Muyuwa and Elka were kept busy, rushing from one hammock to another to blow on the sick people. Many people died. But the people also recognized Elka's power as a witch doctor. They said it wouldn't be long before he was stronger than Muyuwa. Pigs appeared to Elka in dreams, and the next day he would tell the men where to hunt them. The Wai Wai began to depend on Elka as their leader.

Elka decided it was time the people started a new village somewhere else, where the sickness wouldn't follow them. They laughed, thinking of Mistokin and Bahm returning to an empty village. But the night before they were to leave, Elka had a dream. A white man like Bahm appeared to him and said, "Don't go over the high mountains. Stay here." When Elka told the people, they decided they should stay where they were.

Elka became their new chief, and they stayed in their village until Mistokin and Bahm returned a year later. The white men wanted to make God's Paper (what they called the Bible in Wai Wai language) speak to the people in their own language, and they asked Elka to help them. He watched Mistokin and Bahm. He saw them as "different ones" because of the way they lived. He decided to help them, but he and the rest of the Wai Wai still lived in constant fear. Bahm told Elka that the people's badness would have to go before they could forget their fears, and only God had the power to take their badness away.

The more Elka learned about God and His Paper and His Son, the more interested he became. Instead of blowing on sick people, he wondered if he should talk to God about them. He and some of the other people in the village started going to the church services Bahm and Mistokin held each week. But Elka wasn't ready to give up his witchcraft yet. He decided to walk both paths—God's and Kworokyam's. But this couldn't last—soon he would have to make his choice.

One day, as the people were traveling to a party in another village, a young girl named Little Crab became very sick. Her father brought her to Elka, and he blew on her and asked Kworokyam to heal her. But Kworokyam revealed that he would not heal Little Crab. Elka didn't want her to die, so he told her father to take her to Achi, a nurse who had come with Bahm and Mistokin and others who now lived with them. Little Crab died before her father could start the journey.

Little Crab's death caused Elka to begin losing faith in Kworokyam. When Elka became very sick a few days later, he thought he would die. Lying in his hammock, he called out to God, saying, "Father in the sky, this is old Elka talking. Would You be the one to heal me?" He started to feel better that day. He wondered if God had healed him. He began to call on God for healing, like when his two-year-old daughter fell into a campfire and was burned. Instead of using his powers, he took her to the missionaries and prayed for her. He started to realize he had to make a choice. Would he follow Christ or Kworokyam?

One day, Elka asked Bahm about the spirits. He wanted to understand why he could use his powers as a witch doctor to heal before, but now the spirits didn't seem to listen to him. Bahm said:

> The evil spirits heal sometimes, but just to fool us. Kworokyam is the devil's servant. It is his way of getting us to worship him instead of God. God's Paper tells us we can't be followers of Jesus if we serve another. . . . Jesus came to do away with the evil spirits. He came to release us from their power. If you receive Jesus, He will set you free from the spirits' binding cord. But you must choose either Jesus or Kworokyam.

Elka helped translate God's Paper and the words of 1 John 4:18: "There is no fear in love; instead, perfect love drives out fear." He began to talk to the other people about following Jesus, but no one else was interested. Still, Elka couldn't get away from the desire to follow God.

One day, he sat on a log and talked to God, saying:

> Here I am, Father. I'm a witch doctor. This is what I am. I'm a bad person too. I get angry. I scold my wife. And I'm sad about those things. But this is the way I don't want to be. So my old being, take it out, Father. You can because your Son died for my badness, in order to take it away. Fix me to be another kind of person. I want to be like You. . . . Fix me to be like Jesus. That's all I have to say this time, Father.

Over the following days, he started to talk to his people more about Jesus. He led them to pray before eating, thanking God for the food. He wanted God to help the other people to know and trust Him. But there was a test Elka had to pass before the people would believe.

It was a fact that witch doctors who got rid of their charms and stopped performing their witchcraft would soon die. But God's Paper said, "The one who is in you is greater than the one who is in the world" (1 John 4:4). Elka knew the time had come to give up his basket of charms and show that he would follow Jesus only.

But the people, including Elka's wife, were terrified for him. They knew he would die, and they tried over and over to convince him not to get rid of his charms. Elka said, "I'm going to try God to know if He is true. If I die, don't you be receiving Jesus. If I don't die, then you become His companion." This was a test for the people—if Elka didn't die, maybe there was truth in God's Paper. But everyone expected his death.

The people gathered around, and Elka gave his charms to one of the missionaries, called "Kron," a friend of Mistokin and Bahm. Kron told the people not to ask Elka to blow on them. Instead, they should ask him to come and pray to God for them. The people left, fearful and waiting for something bad to happen to Elka. He stood alone in his new faith.

Trials and temptations came. Muyuwa pressured Elka into blowing again, and Elka lied to the missionaries to cover it up. He struggled with pride in his powerful position as chief, and he wanted to trade for and buy things that drew people's attention to him. He discovered that following Jesus didn't mean he would become perfect overnight. He had to choose to obey each day and to confess his sin when he failed.

Other tests came as well. After giving up his charms, nothing happened to him. But the people still weren't convinced to trust God. One day they saw a huge anaconda, and they were sure it was coming to kill Elka. But he remained safe.

Then the wild pigs came back, after being gone from the area for a long time. Elka grabbed his weapons and ran, hoping to kill one. The people tried desperately to stop him. After all, the wild pig was his special animal that appeared to him. These enormous pigs with sharp teeth had killed many people. Surely they would kill Elka now as revenge for him turning his back on them. But he found the pigs and killed two before the others ran off. The people watched as he brought the pigs back to the village and had his wife begin cooking them. They thought somehow he had survived this far, but if he ate the meat of the pig, he would definitely die. The pig in his dream had said he could only eat a tiny part of the back, but Elka was about to eat a large piece of meat. They gathered around, waiting for him to die.

But nothing happened. Elka enjoyed the meat, calling for others to join him.

Finally, the people began to understand: God's power was greater than Kworokyam's. God could drive out their fear with His love.

Over the next few years, many of the Wai Wai people turned to Christ. Even Muyuwa, the evil witch doctor, and at least twelve other witch doctors turned away from following Kworokyam and followed Jesus instead. Elka and other men became elders and preachers in their church.

Elka's wife taught the women about God's Paper. They sang songs like "Jesus Loves Me, God's Paper Says So to Me" (much like our own "Jesus Loves Me"). Realizing the tribes in other parts of the jungle didn't know about Jesus, Elka and others began to make missionary journeys, risking injury and death to share the gospel. They wanted others to know the freedom from fear and badness they had found in Christ, no matter the cost.

Elka spoke to the people, encouraging them to go and spread the gospel, saying, "Jesus came far. So let us go far too."

Because of God's work in Elka's life, many of the Wai Wai people still follow Jesus and have God's Paper, the Bible, in their language today.

SOURCE

Homer E. Dowdy, *Christ's Witchdoctor: From Savage Sorcerer to Jungle Missionary* (New York: Harper & Row, 1963).

Strength to Stand Alone

When Elka gave his life to God and trusted in Jesus, he had to give up his old ways. He was a new creation, what he called a "different one." The people around him, even his own wife, didn't understand why he was turning from witchcraft and following the teaching of God's Paper. He stood alone.

Your life is probably very different from Elka's. I'm guessing you don't face the danger of jaguars and anacondas, and you probably don't hunt spider monkeys and wild pigs. You may never be faced with standing alone like Elka was, leaving behind sorcery and turning to Jesus. But chances are, there will be a time you will have to stand alone. It could be at school or in your neighborhood. It could be with a brother or sister. But every follower of Jesus at times finds himself in situations where he has to choose either to go with the crowd or to stand alone.

Elka learned that God's love drives out fear. It's not that he was fearless, but instead, he learned that God was greater than the things he was afraid of. If God's power was working in Elka, he could stand alone. And when he stood alone, others watched. They waited. They saw God change Elka, and they wanted to be changed too.

The truth that Elka realized is standing alone for God isn't really standing alone at all. The same God who was with Elka is with you. Just as He helped Elka to stand firm and forgave him when he failed, He will help you as well.

Questions

---

1. Elka and the Wai Wai people learned that God's love is different than any love they had known before. Read 1 John 4:9. How does this verse say God showed His love?

2. Look at the next verse, 1 John 4:10. Who loved first, us or God? Why does that matter? Do we have to

do something to make God love us? Did He love Elka because of something Elka did?

3. What about the next verse, 1 John 4:11—what does John say we should do because God loved us?

4. When God changed Elka's life, Elka had to stand alone in obeying Him. How did this show love to his family and friends?

5. Elka saw the missionaries as "different ones," and eventually, he, too, became a "different one." Do you think other people see you as different?

6. When he trusted Jesus, Elka began to see the reason the missionaries could live differently—it wasn't that they were good, but that Jesus was living in them. How does that encourage you?

7. What are some places where you might be asked to stand apart for your faith? When the Wai Wai people began going on missionary journeys, they were risking their lives for the sake of the gospel. Ask God to make Jesus so important to you that you're willing to stand up for Him wherever He places you.

The **ONE** who is in you is **GREATER** than the one who is in the **WORLD**.—1 John 4:4

"Every Christian should live a **GOD**-GUIDED LIFE. If you are not guided by **GOD**, you will be guided by **SOMETHING ELSE**."

Eric Liddell
KNOWING WHAT MATTERS

Eric Liddell's parents were Scottish missionaries to China, where Eric was born on January 16, 1902. It was a dangerous time to live in China with wars and rebellions taking place and missionaries being attacked and sometimes killed. But for Eric, it was home. He spoke the language, ate the food, and felt China, rather than Scotland, was his true home.

When he was six, Eric and his older brother, Rob, were sent to a boarding school in London, where he lived and studied for ten years. His favorite subject was science, and he loved doing scientific experiments. He also spent a lot of time playing sports, like rugby and cricket, and he excelled at running track. He enjoyed sports, but thought of them as an added part of his life, not his reason for living.

While he enjoyed school, being separated from his parents and sister was difficult. He saw them only a few times in twelve years, and it took weeks and even months for letters to be delivered between them. But even though he wasn't with his dad, he grew up wanting to be just like him. From the age of eight or nine, he knew he would be a missionary in China, and he dedicated himself to studying the Bible and preparing to do mission work.

Short for a sprinter at five feet eight inches, Eric had terrible running form. People who saw him run compared him to a "startled deer," a "windmill," and a "terrified ghost." But no one could deny that he was fast. He started competing in races around Scotland and England, and he won most of the races he ran. As he won more and more, he earned prizes made of gold and silver, which he usually gave away as gifts to others.

A friend named DP Thomson was traveling around Scotland, sharing the gospel with workers and townspeople. DP reached out to Eric and asked if he might go with him to speak to some factory workers, and Eric agreed, but not without some fear. He was nervous to stand before them and later said it was the bravest thing he had ever done. He talked to the people about his running and his faith and how the two fit together.

This was a turning point. Eric began to travel and speak to more groups, and as his fame on the track grew, so did the size of the crowds who came to hear him speak. He didn't feel qualified to preach, but thought if God called him to it, God would supply him with the necessary power.

As he continued to train and compete, he got faster and faster, breaking records and defying odds. In one of his most famous races, Eric was competing in the 440-yard distance. Just a few feet into the race, his foot was clipped, and he was pushed over by another runner. He fell into the grass beside the track and then, thinking his fall disqualified him from the race, watched the other runners continue. He heard his coach yelling at him to get up and run again, but he continued to sit until a race official told him he could compete. He was twenty yards behind the other runners, a seemingly impossible distance to make up. But he took off, chasing them down gradually, cutting the lead bit by bit. In the end, he passed the other runners and won by a six-yard margin. Then, he collapsed onto the track, having given every bit of himself to the race. The crowd couldn't believe what they'd seen, and word about Eric Liddell began to spread around Scotland and the rest of the United Kingdom.

Eric began preparing for the 1924 Olympic Games, which would be held in Paris the year he turned twenty-two. He planned to run the 100- and 200-meter races and the 4x100- and 4x400-meter relays. But then a problem came up.

Early on, Eric had determined not to compete on Sundays. He believed Sunday should be devoted to God, so he spent his Sundays in church, often preaching, instead of racing. But when the Olympic track schedule came out, he discovered the 100-meter and both of the relay races would require him to run on Sunday. Most people assumed he would make an exception this time.

Surely for the Olympics he would choose to run, just this once. Eric wouldn't compromise, though. He said, "Each one comes to the cross-roads at some period of his life and must make his decision for or against His Master." He would run the 400-meter race instead.

When people found out he refused to run, many were angry with him. They couldn't understand why he wouldn't run just this once. Crowds came to his door and yelled, "He's a traitor to his country." People said he wasn't built for the 400 meters and didn't stand a chance at winning. He wasn't tall or springy enough, and he might not be able to last in a race that much longer than what he normally ran.

Regardless of what happened, Eric wanted to compete honorably. If he lost, he would do so knowing he had done his best. But he wanted to win. He was asked once how he won so many races, even when people thought he couldn't win. He answered, "I don't like to be beaten." His competitive nature and desire to do his best, no matter what, propelled him past other runners.

Finally, the Olympics began. Eric's first race was the 200 meters. He ran well, enough to earn the bronze medal, but not fast enough to be a threat to the runners expected to do well in the 400 meters. In his 400-meter qualifying races, he ran fast enough to advance to the finals, but slow enough to have to run in the outside lane. Because of this positioning, he wouldn't know if he was in front or behind until later in the race.

The evening of Friday, July 11, 1924, Eric and the other runners warmed up before taking their places along the track. As he did before every race, Eric walked along and shook hands with each of the other runners, then took his starting position. The gun went off to begin the race, and Eric was fastest off the starting line. The runners watching him take the lead thought he would soon run out of steam, that he had gone out too fast and wouldn't be able to keep up his pace. Even Eric was asking himself if he could keep pushing himself that quickly. But he pushed on. He won by a length of six yards, a huge margin in a 400-meter race, and broke the world record in the process.

The British team hoisted Eric onto their shoulders, parading him along. He went from being "a traitor to his country" to being, as newspapers called him, "one of the most popular men in Paris." His fame followed him, with crowds greeting him at the train station in Scotland and large audiences coming to hear him preach. He was quick to point out that winning isn't what's most important, but rather, it's doing your best that matters.

"There are many men and women who have done their best, but who have not succeeded in gaining the laurels of victory," he said to one crowd. "To them, as much honor is due as to those who have received those laurels."

Because Eric was so famous after the Olympics, people couldn't understand why he would give up everything to move to China. But since he had been a boy, he had planned to go back "home" and work as a missionary, like his father. Not even being an Olympic champion could change those plans. People would ask him why he was going, and he would respond, "Because I believe God made me for China."

In China, Eric would run a different kind of race. He studied the Bible, taught school, and prepared for mission work. He married a woman named Florence, and they had two daughters. Just like when he was growing up in China, the situation there was not good. Missionaries were kidnapped and sometimes killed. World War II was raging, with Japan invading and killing millions of Chinese men, women, and children.

As the situation grew worse, Eric and Florence had to separate so that she and the girls could stay safe. They went to Toronto, Canada, while Eric stayed behind. Florence was going to give birth again, this time without Eric there. He got his family settled on the ship that would take them to Canada, said goodbye, and walked away, hoping it wouldn't be long before they saw each other again.

But then Sunday, December 7, 1941, came. The Japanese bombed American planes stationed at Pearl Harbor in Hawaii. Because he was a foreigner, Eric was placed under house arrest and later taken with other foreigners to an "internment camp," much like a prison. The Japanese soldiers set up the camp so they could watch over the prisoners and make sure they didn't cause trouble or help the Chinese. During the two and a half years that prisoners were kept at the camp, the number of captives reached up to 1,800 at a time before they were liberated by Allied forces.

Living in the camp changed many things, but it didn't change who Eric Liddell was. He woke early in the morning, while everyone else slept, and prayed for an hour. At night, he would study his Bible and then spend more time in prayer, praying for his family, his fellow camp residents, and the guards keeping them captive.

Eric spent 694 days in this camp, and he was loved by everyone. One fellow prisoner said, "Every day to [Eric] was still precious. He threw himself into it to make others feel better about the situation all of us were in." He preached, organized sports days, did extra chores to help others, and taught Bible, math, and science. Other prisoners came to him with their problems and questions, and he listened and loved them well. He didn't complain, and he didn't talk about people behind their backs. To many of the younger prisoners, he was known as "Uncle Eric."

Having studied the teaching of Jesus, Eric thought and taught a lot on the passage that says, "Love your enemies, do what is good to those who hate you, bless those who curse you, pray for those who mistreat you" (Luke 6:26–28). He encouraged the people in the camp to pray for the camp guards. He told those who listened to him teach, "I've begun to pray for the guards, and it's changed my whole attitude toward them. When we hate them we are self-centered."

Eric didn't want to be self-centered; instead, he wanted to serve others. By doing this, he knew he was really serving God. So, he served in every imaginable way, until he couldn't serve anymore.

On their occasional "sports days," prisoners would play different sports and games, and some of the young men would challenge Eric to a race. He was older now and hadn't trained in years, but he still left the competition in his dust, even when he gave the other runners a head start.

But one day, he lost. He ran as hard as he could, but it wasn't enough. Having lost a lot of weight from the lack of food in the camp, he was growing weaker. Most people thought it was just because of the camp conditions, but something was actually very wrong with Eric. He was confused, exhausted, and dizzy.

Too sick to stand and walk, he ended up in the camp hospital. The doctors thought he would get over whatever was making him sick, but instead, he got worse. On February 21, 1945, he was strong enough to get up and walk; then he came back to bed and wrote to Florence. Suddenly, his condition worsened, and he had two strokes, which damaged his brain. A few hours later, Eric died. He was forty-three years old.

The camp mourned for Eric, lining the road for his funeral and crying as they talked to one another about how much he had meant to them. At his funeral service, they sang his favorite hymn, "Be Still My Soul," one verse of which says:

> Be still, my soul, the Lord is on thy side;
>
> Bear patiently the cross of grief or pain.
>
> Leave to thy God to order and provide;
>
> In every change, He faithful will remain.
>
> Be still, my soul, thy best, thy heavenly friend
>
> Through thorny ways, leads to a joyful end.
>
> —Katharina von Schlegel

Eric's best Friend had been with him through the camp, carrying him as he worked and served and then bringing him to his joyful home in heaven. After he died, the doctors discovered Eric had a brain tumor. It wasn't just the camp conditions that had weakened him; he had been suffering from a tumor, probably for years, without knowing it.

But his soul was calm and comforted in the Lord. He had run his race with faith and perseverance, and because of his faithfulness, hundreds of lives in the camp were changed.

SOURCE

Duncan Hamilton, *For the Glory: The Untold and Inspiring Story of Eric Liddell, Hero of "Chariots of Fire"* (New York: Penguin, 2016).

Strength in Knowing What Matters

For many people, Eric Liddell is a hero because he's an Olympic champion. He stayed true to his principles by not running on Sunday, and he still won an Olympic gold medal in world record time. But it's what Eric did after the Olympics that is most heroic. He gave up fame, money, comfort, and a chance at future Olympic gold medals, all because he believed God had designed him for a different life.

Many people in his circumstances would have spent their days in the camp thinking, *What if? What if I had stayed in Scotland and been a runner and a preacher? What if I had gone with my family to Canada?* Or some of us would have been tempted to talk about our greatness, wanting others to serve us.

But Eric didn't talk about his Olympic glory with those who knew him as "Uncle Eric." Instead, he listened to *their* stories, comforted them, and served them. He was able to do these things because his strength did not come from himself, but from God. He spent time each morning and each night praying and studying his Bible. He knew without these things he would be empty, unable to give what people needed from him.

His life inspired hundreds of people who lived in the camp, some of whom went on to become missionaries like him. His daughters grew up missing their dad, but thankful for his life and legacy. Eric knew what truly mattered in life—not the glory and fame that fade away, but the unfading glory of God.

Questions

---

1. Read Matthew 5:1–12. This was one of Eric Liddell's favorite Bible passages. How did he live according to the things Jesus taught in these verses?

2. When he read the Sermon on the Mount, the passage that these verses come from, Eric said, "The first time you read it you feel that it is impossible. The second time you feel that nothing else is possible." What do you think he meant by this?

3. Eric knew what truly mattered in life, and he lived his life with purpose. But people didn't understand

the choice he made to give up fame and fortune. Have you ever been misunderstood because of a choice you made to follow God's path? How did that feel, or how do you think it would feel if you did?

4. Is there any area in your life where you are living by what others think is important, instead of what God says is important? If so, pray that God will remind you of what really matters and that He will help you live a life that reflects that.

This is how we have come to know LOVE: He laid down HIS LIFE for us. We should also LAY DOWN our lives for our brothers and sisters.
—1 John 3:16

"My memory is nearly gone,

but I remember two things:

That I am a GREAT SINNER
and that CHRIST is a GREAT SAVIOR."

John Newton
GODLY AMBITION

On July 24, 1725, in London, England, Elizabeth Newton gave birth to a boy, who was named John after his father. The elder John Newton was the captain of merchant ships that traded in ports around the Mediterranean Sea. The younger John didn't know his father well since he was often away sailing. After his mother died when he was six years old, John's father married again, and soon after, young John was sent away to boarding school.

By the time he was eleven, John had completed his time in school (most children did not study past this age) and was making his first voyage as a sailor. He spent the next several years sailing, often spending his time on shore with wild friends, drinking and getting into trouble. He had two near-death experiences: once he was thrown from a horse and nearly landed on a sharp spike, and the other time he was a few minutes too late to get on a boat that later sank, causing most of the men on board to drown. Both of these close calls caused him to turn to the Bible and religion, but it wasn't true faith and didn't last.

John was known for being arrogant and harsh. Other sailors didn't like him, and he didn't respect his commanding officers. On one ship, he wrote a song that mocked the captain and taught it to the other sailors. In his desire to soothe his guilt over his sin and to get others to approve of him, he convinced them to join in his actions.

While on board a ship bound for Sierra Leone in Africa, John met a slave trader named Amos Clow. Clow made money by owning a "factory," which was a fort where Africans were kept after being captured by slave hunters. Clow would hold these men, women, and children in his factory until slave ships landed. Then he would trade humans in exchange for goods. The humans were taken on board the ships to endure the Middle

Passage—the route from Africa, to be sold in America or the West Indies.

When he met Amos Clow, John was twenty-four years old and anxious to earn money. Hearing Clow's stories of wealth and adventure, John decided he would stay with Clow in Africa rather than continue sailing. So he agreed to work for Clow as a slave trader. But what he hoped would be his ticket to fortune actually led to his own slavery. John ended up sick, starving, and often in chains. He was falsely accused of stealing, and Clow punished him greatly.

As he was planting lime trees in Clow's orchard one day, slaving in the brutal heat, Clow passed by and sarcastically said, "Who knows that by the time these trees grow up and bear, you may go home to England, obtain the command of a ship, and return to reap the fruits of your labors? We see strange things sometimes happen." Clow said this as a joke, meaning to show John just how hopeless his situation was, but his words actually turned out to be true.

Eventually, John was able to get off the island, but the ship on which he sailed home to England was badly damaged in a storm. Once again, John nearly died. In his distress, he called out to God. Slowly, he was beginning to see that God loved him. He began to pray and believed God could hear him. But it was just the beginning of his journey to fully trusting God.

A friend of his father gave John the opportunity to sail back to Africa, this time as second-in-command of a slave ship. He did end up eating limes from the trees he had planted years before. Slaves and factory owners who had known him as a sick and starving young man were shocked to see him return as a slave trader. For the next several years, John sailed as first mate then as captain back and forth from England to Africa to the West Indies and America. His job was to trade for kidnapped slaves in Africa, then chain them in the ship and sail across the Atlantic Ocean to the ports where they would be sold. Many slaves got sick and died on the Middle Passage. They were kept in chains through the whole journey, cramped together below deck.

As John continued reading the Bible and learning about God, he began leading the ship's crew in worship services on Sundays. He grew to understand grace and that it was the work of Jesus, not our own good works, that saves people. But like most British people during the time, he had no doubts about the slave trade. His growing faith didn't cause him to question whether he should be involved in selling human beings. At least, not yet.

After he married his wife, Polly, John started thinking about finding a job where he could be home with her instead of traveling. He got a job with the government, but something in his heart was stirring him to become a preacher. God had changed his life from the rebellious wanderings of his childhood and teenage years to his being treated as a slave in Africa to seeing the goodness and grace of his Savior. He wanted to serve others and tell them the good news.

In the process of working to become a pastor, John wrote a book about his experiences. It quickly became a best seller in England and was published in other countries as well. People were excited to read about the radical change that had taken place in this man's life. When he became the pastor of a church in Olney, a town sixty miles north of London, many people came to hear this famous author preach, but his ministry was mostly to the poor residents of Olney. He started a children's ministry and a prayer group, and he spent many hours each week teaching from the Bible.

With his friend, a poet named William Cowper (pronounced "Cooper"), John began writing hymns for his church. He knew that music helped people learn, so he would sometimes write a hymn to go along with the sermon he was preaching. This was how he came to write a hymn for his church to sing on New Year's Day in 1773. His sermon was on the prayer of King David in 1 Chronicles 17:16–17, which says:

> Who am I, Lord God, and what is my house that you have brought me this far? . . . You regard me as a man of distinction, Lord God.

The words of this prayer are echoed in the words of John's hymn, which you've probably sung before:

> Amazing grace! (how sweet the sound)
>
> That saved a wretch like me!
>
> I once was lost, but now am found;
>
> Was blind, but now I see.

After fifteen years in Olney, John and Polly moved to London, where John became pastor at St. Mary Woolnoth Church. Being in London brought him in contact with many people, including a young man named William Wilberforce. John had known William as a young boy, but now he was in his twenties and serving as a member of Parliament, the group of British lawmakers. Much like John, William had spent several years running around, drinking and gambling. But by God's grace, he had come to know Christ, and now he was confused about what to do with his life.

As a new Christian, William wondered if God might want him to leave Parliament and become a pastor instead. John advised William to stay in Parliament and serve God there, right where he already was. John later wrote in a letter about William, "I hope the Lord will make him a blessing, both as a Christian and as a statesman."

Neither John nor William had any idea how right that hope would turn out to be. Thanks to John's counsel, William remained in Parliament, where he took on the cause of abolishing the British slave trade. With other abolitionists, like

Hannah More, Thomas Clarkson, and Olaudah Equiano, William Wilberforce worked for years to convince those in Parliament to vote for his proposal to end the slave trade. Year after year, his proposal was defeated.

Over time, John Newton came to see the evils of the slave trade. He deeply regretted participating in it. In 1788, he wrote a short booklet called *Thoughts upon the African Slave Trade*. Because so many people in Parliament were wealthy from the trade—some owned ships; others had sugar plantations in the West Indies—it was not easy to change their minds and convince them to end it. John hoped that writing his firsthand experiences might help people see the horrors of what truly happened on those ships.

He wrote, "I hope it will always be a subject of humiliating reflection to me that I was once an active instrument in a business at which my heart now shudders." He went on to describe in detail what a slave experienced, from kidnapping to being chained to sickness to torture. A copy of the booklet was sent to every member of Parliament. People all over England read it, and it caused many to change their minds about the slave trade.

After twenty years of defeats in Parliament, in February 1807, William Wilberforce's bill passed, abolishing the slave trade. That December, eighty-two-year-old John Newton passed away.

Before his death, John wrote the inscription that was to go on his tomb:

JOHN NEWTON

ONCE AN INFIDEL AND LIBERTINE

A SERVANT OF SLAVES IN AFRICA

WAS

BY THE RICH MERCY OF OUR LORD AND

SAVIOUR

JESUS CHRIST

PRESERVED, RESTORED, PARDONED

AND APPOINTED TO PREACH THE FAITH

HE HAD LONG LABOURED TO DESTROY

SOURCE

Jonathan Aitken, *John Newton: From Disgrace to Amazing Grace* (Wheaton, IL: Crossway, 2007).

Strength in Ambition

When we hear someone described as having ambition, we think of a desire for fame or power or achievement. An ambitious person is someone who is willing to work very hard to reach their goals and get what they want. This definitely describes John Newton, who worked his way up from a sailor to a ship's captain, finding a way to earn plenty of money in the slave trade.

But there's a difference between worldly ambition and godly ambition. For most of his early years, John Newton cared only about himself and what he wanted, and he was willing to do whatever he needed to in order to get it. Everything changed, though, when God showed him His amazing grace and saved him. As he grew in his faith and read the Bible, John began to understand what it meant to have godly ambition. This new ambition led him to become a pastor, where he served the factory workers, blacksmiths, lace makers, and other poor people in Olney and London.

It was godly ambition that led William Wilberforce to stay in Parliament and work hard for twenty years to see the slave trade abolished. And it was godly ambition that caused John Newton to write about the horrible things he had seen and done in his years as a slave trader.

Sometimes people think, *God can't possibly use me to do His work. I've done too many bad things.* John Newton shared his story freely because he didn't want people to think they were too bad for God to change them and use them in His kingdom. If God could save a "wretch" like John, as he wrote in the song, then He could save anyone.

No matter what your past is like and no matter how you mess up in the future, God's amazing grace is for you. And the talents and passions He's given you are no accident. He wants to strengthen you and give you a godly ambition to use those things for His glory.

Questions

---

1. Read Philippians 2:3–4. What can these verses teach us about the difference between worldly ambition and godly ambition?

2. Now read verses 5–11. Jesus is our example of godly ambition. What does that kind of ambition look like, according to this passage?

3. What's easier—worldly ambition or godly ambition? Is it easier for you to look out for yourself or for others?

4. Who is someone you've seen serving others instead of just doing what might serve himself (or herself)?

5. When you think about your own dreams and plans for your life—both now and in the future—have you thought about how God can strengthen you to help and serve others? What might that look like in your own life?

"For even the SON OF MAN did not come to be served, but to SERVE, and to GIVE his life as a ransom for MANY."
–Mark 10:45

"I feel a **BURNING DESIRE** that **ALL** the world may **KNOW GOD**."

William Carey
HUMILITY

Born in England in 1761, William Carey was the son of a village schoolteacher. He spent most of his free time in nature, exploring the forest and carefully inspecting insects, birds, flowers, and trees. William had an adventurous spirit, listening closely to his uncle's tales of pioneering in Canada and reading Captain James Cook's travel logs about his discovery of the Pacific islands.

When he was fourteen, he was apprenticed to a shoemaker for seven years of training. One day, he lied to his master about money. He prayed that God would excuse him and that he wouldn't get caught, promising he would never do it again. But William's master and the whole village found out about his dishonesty. His guilt led him to see how much he needed a Savior, and he asked God for mercy and forgiveness and began following Christ.

William became a man while British troops were in America, fighting the Revolutionary War, and while William Wilberforce was fighting in British Parliament to abolish slavery. From an early age, William Carey hated slavery. As it continued, he protested by refusing to purchase and use sugar, which was produced by slaves. He saw the dignity of all people, and his heart was soft to those who were suffering.

As he continued to grow in his knowledge of God, William began preaching in local churches. For over three years, he walked twelve miles to preach every other Sunday at a church that had no pastor. He loved the Bible and wanted others to love it also. But it wasn't enough for William that people in England should know God. The more he studied Captain James Cook's logbooks and maps of the world, the more compassion he felt for those who had never heard of God's love for them. In his writing, Captain Cook described people on the islands he had visited, and a fire was lit in

William's heart to go to those places with the good news about Jesus.

At this time, though, English churches weren't interested in sending missionaries. As William began writing and talking about his vision for England to spread the gospel around the world, some pastors thought he was being foolish. They believed there was enough work to do in their own country—why would they send people and money to other places? William wrote a pamphlet that was printed and sent to churches. He called for people to end their love of money and comfort and instead to obey the command of Jesus to go into all the world and make disciples.

In 1792, William preached at a meeting of church leaders from several churches that were partners with his own. His message came to be known as "the deathless sermon" because for more than two hundred years people have been quoting William's words. He preached from Isaiah 54 about spreading wide the tent and extending the gospel to those around the world who had never heard it. He spoke about God's power giving His people the strength they needed, and he said these famous words that have been repeated for generations: "Expect great things from God. Attempt great things for God."

The pastors who listened thought it was a good sermon, but they still weren't ready to send out missionaries. William cried out to one of the leaders, Andrew Fuller, and said, "Is there nothing again going to be done, sir?" The pastors talked and decided to prepare a plan for sending missionaries out from England.

A year later, William and his family boarded a ship headed for India. He was the first to be sent by the newly formed Baptist Missionary Society. The voyage lasted for five months, sailing past Europe, Africa, and parts of Asia. Their first home in India was in a jungle that was known for its cobras, pythons, crocodiles, leopards, and tigers. The Indian people were terrified of the tigers because they had seen many friends and family members dragged off and eaten by the fierce cats. But William and his family settled there, building a house out of bamboo. It wasn't long, though, before he was asked to move to a different part of India. So, William and his family packed up and set off again.

William lived and worked in India for the next forty years until his death in 1834. He eventually settled with three other missionaries in Calcutta, where they built schools and William taught at a local college. The heart of his work, though, was translating the Bible into Indian languages. He believed every person needed God's Word in his or her own language. There were many different languages in India, so William set to work on several of them. He knew the people of India would be reached with the gospel only if other Indians could explain it to them and teach them what the Bible said. So, he devoted most of his life to learning languages and working with people who spoke them so that he could have more and more Bibles printed.

When he died, William had translated the whole Bible into six languages, and the New Testament into more than twenty. These Bibles were printed on the missionaries' own printing press and were sent out with British, American, and Indian missionaries to different parts of the country and the surrounding nations, like Nepal.

Even though he accomplished so many good things in his life, William didn't think highly of himself. He once wrote that if God could use *him*, He could use anyone. And he said, "I am not one of those who are 'strong and do exploits,'" (a reference to Daniel 11:32). He compared himself to his fellow missionaries and thought they were far better than he was. But he also knew that other people spoke highly of him, praising him back in England for his work. He wrote a letter to a pastor friend in England, saying:

I have long made the language of Psalm 51 my own. "Have mercy upon me, O God, according unto the multitude of thy tender mercies blot out my transgressions." Should you outlive me, and have any influence to prevent it, I earnestly request that no epithets of praise may ever accompany my name, such as "the faithful servant of God," etc. All such expressions would convey a falsehood. To me belong shame and confusion of face. I can only say, "Hangs my helpless soul on Thee."

Only William knew just how much he needed God's strength. Other people looked at him and saw a faithful man, but he wanted them to know it was only God's faithful love that was helping him to live well and work hard.

This help was needed more than ever when loved ones died or when a fire destroyed much of the translation work he had done. He prayed for

God's strength when the local government began persecuting the missionaries and when there were arguments between older and younger missionaries. God was faithful again and again.

William didn't just work on translation and teaching, though. He also worked in his large garden. Ever since he was a young boy, he had loved being in nature. He was no different in India. He had seeds and bulbs brought from England so he could plant them, and he collected flowers and plants from other parts of India to include in his garden. He spent hours walking through the garden, working in the dirt, and enjoying God's creation.

But it wasn't just plants that he enjoyed; he also loved creatures. As his sons grew older and were sent out to different parts of Asia, William would write and ask them to send him plants and animals from where they were living. His son Jabez sent him bright parakeets, cockatoos, birds of paradise, a cassowary, and a type of kangaroo. He asked another son for lizards, snakes, frogs, and monkeys. He built aviaries for the birds and enjoyed walking around and hearing their songs.

For William, being in nature was a way of enjoying God. He didn't go to India just to tell people they needed to trust Jesus so they wouldn't be punished; he went to share God's love and glory with them and to invite them to enjoy God too. Spending time with plants and animals was William's way of celebrating God's creativity and beauty.

Spending time in nature also helped build William's humility. It's hard to gaze on God's amazing creation and think of ourselves as being important and worthy of praise. When William saw the intricate design of a butterfly's wings or the bright colors of a parakeet or when he watched a monkey skillfully slinging himself from tree to tree, he praised God as the only One truly worthy of honor and praise. Because of that and his own sinful thoughts and attitudes, he knew how much he needed his Savior, Jesus.

This humility was what caused him, when he was near death, to say these words to a friend who had been talking about William's life and legacy: "Mr. Duff, you have been speaking about Dr. Carey, Dr. Carey; when I am gone, say nothing about Dr. Carey—speak about Dr. Carey's Saviour."

When William died, there were then fourteen British missionary societies, as well as similar groups in America and other countries. Even today, thousands of missionaries are sent out by organizations like the one William Carey started. Because of his patience and passion, the gospel continues to go out to people who have never heard the name of Jesus. But William would be quick to remind us that it is not he who matters, but instead his Savior, Jesus Christ.

SOURCE
S. Pearce Carey, *William Carey* (London: Wakeman Trust, 2008).

Strength in Humility

C. S. Lewis, author of the Chronicles of Narnia book series and many other books, once wrote about humility. He said that a truly humble man "will not be thinking about humility; he will not be thinking about himself at all." We see this in William Carey's life. It wasn't his own desire to do something great that compelled him to start a missionary society and move to India. He wasn't thinking of himself—he was thinking of the Great Commission given by Jesus to go into all the world and preach the gospel, and he was thinking about all the people around the world who hadn't yet heard that message.

Have you ever eaten an amazing food and couldn't wait to tell people about it? Or maybe you played a fun game or read a great book and just had to talk about it with a friend. This is what William Carey's relationship with God was like.

He enjoyed God so much and was so thankful for His Son's sacrificial love that he just had to tell people about it. It broke his heart that other people didn't know. How would they know Him if no one told them?

But when he went to India, William didn't stop enjoying God. He didn't think of life as two columns—the important stuff on one side and the unimportant stuff on the other. Gardening was as important as translation; studying nature was as needed as preaching. This is because he saw all of life as worship.

Have you ever thought of playing a sport as worship? You're using the body God gave you to compete and play and have fun. What about drawing a picture or making up a song? You're being like God, who gave us His creativity and loves to see us use it. Even cleaning your room can be an act of worship because you're putting things in order just as God gives things their purpose and place.

When we begin to think of these things as worship, it helps us live with humility. Having people tell us how great we are at a sport or music or school isn't important to us when we think of our lives as pointing to God. When we're spending our days enjoying God and His gifts to us, we won't be as concerned about hearing our names praised; instead, we'll want everyone to know this great God who loves us.

Questions

1. Read Matthew 28:16–20. What command does Jesus give His followers?

2. Look again at verse 20. What promise does He make?

3. How does His promise help us to obey His command?

4. How do these verses go with William Carey's encouragement that Christians should "expect great things from God; attempt great things for God"? Who should get the glory when God does great things through His people?

5. Read Psalm 34:8. What does the writer tell us to do? How can you do it today?

TASTE and see that the LORD is **GOOD**. How happy is the person who takes **REFUGE** in him!
–Psalm 34:8

"I felt such **LOVE** and **JOY** as my **TONGUE** was not able to **EXPRESS**."

George Liele
COMPASSION

Born around 1750 in Virginia, where his parents, Nancy and Liele, were slaves, George Liele was originally just called George. We don't know much about his childhood, except that his father loved God and probably taught his son about his faith.

In 1764, a farmer named Henry Sharp moved his family from Virginia to Georgia. They brought nine slaves with them, including George, who was around fourteen years old. Eventually, George was given the last name of his master, so he was known as George Sharp.

Henry Sharp was a Tory, which meant he took the side of the British leading up to and during the Revolutionary War. Some of the colonists in Georgia didn't like this, and they also didn't like that he supported a church having a pastor who wasn't white. But Sharp did things his own way. He and his brother-in-law, a preacher named

Matthew Moore, started a Baptist church in the early 1770s.

The Sharp family taught George to read and write, and he attended the Baptist church. George later wrote about his faith:

> I was informed both by white and black
> people that my father was the only black
> person who knew the Lord in a spiritual
> way in that country (Virginia). I always
> had a natural fear of God from my youth
> and was often checked in conscience
> with thoughts of death which barred
> me from many sins and bad company. I
> knew no other way at that time to hope
> for salvation but only in the perfor-
> mance of good works.

Even from a young age, George knew about God and felt bad about sinning. But he believed he could only be saved by God if he did lots of good things. When he was in his early twenties, something changed. He listened to the preaching in church and realized he wasn't a Christian. He read the Bible and prayed, while learning more about the good news of Jesus in church, and saw that his own good deeds could never save him. Only the work of Jesus Christ could do that. George prayed and asked Jesus to save him and to give him work to do for God—not to earn His love, but to show Him love.

When he had given his life to God, he wrote, "I felt such love and joy as my tongue was not able to express." He no longer felt pressure to do enough good deeds to save himself. He had seen that this was impossible. Only trusting in the death and resurrection of Jesus could save him from the punishment he deserved for his sin. This was true freedom.

George then stood in the church and told the other members how God had saved him, and Matthew Moore baptized him in the nearby creek. And just as he had asked in his prayer, God gave him work to do. George began teaching fellow slaves about God, wanting them to have the same joy and love he had.

He started out teaching people hymns—songs about God. He encouraged the people on the plantation to sing, and he explained what the songs meant. As he did this, he taught them about who God is and what His Word says.

When the white members of the church saw George's talent at teaching, they decided to allow him to preach to slaves in the church. Soon after this, the church ordained him as the first black Baptist pastor in America, and they sent him out to preach wherever he could gather slaves together, not just in the church but also in fields and barns and under trees. George also preached to the white members of his church, an action that was extremely rare in the 1700s, when sadly, many people considered African Americans to be inferior and less intelligent than white people.

One of the plantations where George preached as a guest was called Silver Bluff, where a Baptist church had been started for the slaves owned by a man named George Galphin. When slave owners allowed preachers to come and teach their slaves, most of the time they did so because they wanted the preachers to tell the slaves that God wanted them to obey their masters and work hard. But Galphin seems to have been different. At Silver Bluff, George Sharp (Liele) didn't preach about obeying masters but about Matthew 11:28, which says, "Come to me, all of you who are weary and burdened, and I will give you rest."

After the sermon, a slave named David George went to George Sharp and told him how he felt weary and burdened and needed Jesus to give him rest. Soon after, David George became the pastor of the Silver Bluff Baptist Church, and he and George remained connected through the rest of their lives.

When the war came in 1776, Henry Sharp fought for the British Empire as an officer. He freed George from slavery, and George then changed his name to take his father's name as his last name, becoming George Liele. With his wife, Hannah, and their four children, George moved to Savannah, Georgia, where he was joined by David George. The two men went around farming and preaching the gospel to slaves. But when Henry Sharp was killed in the war, some of his children tried to re-enslave George, claiming that their father hadn't actually freed him. They had him arrested and put in jail, but he was released when he showed the papers proving his freedom.

Like his former master, George took the British side in the war. Things were more and more dangerous for him in Savannah, so in 1782 he and his family sailed to Kingston, Jamaica, with Colonel Kirkland, a British officer who loaned George $700 to pay for the voyage. To pay him back, George worked as an indentured servant for Kirkland for two years.

As he looked around Jamaica, George saw the terrible treatment of slaves at the hands of their British masters. He started preaching to the slaves, but some government and religious leaders didn't like this. They threw him in jail, where his feet were held in stocks. It was against the law of the British Empire to preach the gospel to slaves, but when he was released from jail, George went right on preaching.

George was the first-known Baptist missionary. He took the gospel to Jamaica ten years before William Carey went to India and started a modern missions movement. Unlike many missionaries today, George had no mission agency to send him to Jamaica or to give money to his family. Instead, he worked as a farmer to provide a home and food for his wife and children. He built a church and a free school for black children. He was continually persecuted by British officials who didn't want him preaching. Every sermon he preached and every prayer he prayed in his church had to be written and checked by authorities before he could speak it to his congregation. The government and other religious leaders wanted to be sure he wasn't preaching anything that would stir the slaves up to fight against their masters.

The message he preached of freedom in Christ soothed the hearts of many slaves. He gave them hope and taught them of a Savior who promised rest for those who were tired and weary.

But his impact wasn't felt just in Savannah and Jamaica. David George, who had grown in his knowledge of God by working with George Liele, established the first Baptist church in Canada and later moved to Sierra Leone in West Africa and started a church there.

In 1791, George Liele wrote a letter to Dr. John Rippon, a leader in the British Baptist Missionary Society in London, telling him about his life in America and his current work in Jamaica. He told him that he had baptized 400 people in Jamaica and that his church had around 350 members, including a few white people. He asked for the British Baptists' help with money to build a church building, which they agreed to. He asked for British missionaries to come join him in his work, and some did. These missionaries came to Jamaica and saw the cruel treatment of the slaves, and they told people back home in England what they saw. This testimony was helpful in abolishing the British slave trade. Today, George Liele is considered one of the men who worked to gain independence for Jamaica.

After visiting London for six years in the 1820s, George Liele died in 1828. He left behind money and property to care for his family. But more important, he left a legacy of slaves and former slaves who knew freedom and rest in Jesus Christ because of his faithful teaching.

SOURCE

David T. Shannon, Julia Frazier White, and Deborah Bingham Van Broekhoven, eds., *George Liele's Life and Legacy: An Unsung Hero* (Macon, GA: Mercer University Press, 2012).

Strength in Compassion

While George Liele seems to have had a kind master and was given unusual freedom and opportunity as a slave, it's still certain that he faced persecution and felt heavy burdens because of his condition. Being enslaved meant he was seen as having less worth than free people. To be owned by another person means you aren't free to make your own decisions—to go where you want, to do what you want, to say what you want. And even though his situation was better than many, he still looked around and saw his brothers and sisters suffering under harsh masters.

For a man whose life's purpose was to work hard for his master, it makes sense that George would think the same way of God. He thought he needed to work hard to earn his salvation. If he just did enough good deeds, perhaps God would love him and choose to save him from the punishment he deserved for his sin.

But when he heard the gospel preached in church, he realized he was thinking about it all wrong. God didn't require him to do enough good things to cover up the bad things. George saw that if this was what God wanted, he was doomed. No one can be perfect. None of us can pay for our sins with enough goodness. We're sinful in our hearts.

Instead, George saw in the Bible that Jesus came to take that burden away from us and to give us rest. And the rest He gives us is rest from trying to earn God's love. When God sent Jesus to pay the penalty for our sin, He showed us that we already have His love. If we had to earn it, we would be hopeless. But He gives it to us freely—it's a gift!

As George went around to preach to slaves, he shared this gift with them. And when he preached to the white people in church, he shared the gift with them as well. Everyone is equal before God. We're all sinners in need of His saving grace.

This is the message George brought to Jamaica, and it brought hope and dignity to people who were treated terribly. This message led the slaves in Jamaica to stand up against their harsh treatment and, eventually, gain freedom and independence from those who thought they were fit only to be slaves.

While your life probably looks very different from George's, the truth is everyone who hasn't trusted Christ is a slave to sin. When you show God's love to other people—friends, neighbors, siblings—you get to offer them freedom from trying to do enough good things to earn that love. God can give you the courage and compassion to tell others that He already loves them and wants them to trust Him. And God's love can also strengthen you to have compassion for those who are treated badly and courage to work to see justice done.

Questions

1. How would you define the word *compassion*? (Feel free to use a dictionary.)

2. Read Matthew 11:28–30, the passage that George Liele preached from. How does Jesus show compassion through these words He spoke?

3. George Liele learned he couldn't come to Jesus Christ through his own good works. Instead, he needed to trust in the work of Jesus in his place. Do you ever feel like God will love you only if you do enough good things? What does Ephesians 2:8–9 say about that?

4. Sometimes when we see someone suffering or being treated unjustly, we think, *That's not my problem*. That's what the priest and the Levite did in the parable of the good Samaritan in Luke 10:30–37. But what does verse 33 say about the Samaritan?

5. Samaritans and Jews didn't get along. In fact, the Samaritans were looked down on and hated by the Jews. But this Samaritan had such compassion that he went out of his way to help the injured Jewish man. God can give you that kind of compassion too. Whom might He want you to show compassion to this week?

He **COMFORTS** us in all our affliction, so that we may be able to comfort those who are in **ANY** kind of affliction, through the comfort we ourselves receive from **GOD**.

—2 Corinthians 1:4

"He is NO FOOL who GIVES what he CANNOT KEEP to GAIN what he CANNOT LOSE."

Jim Elliot
SACRIFICIAL LOVE

Jim Elliot, who was later called a "picture of speed, fury, and recklessness" by a childhood friend, was born in Portland, Oregon, in 1927. His father, Fred, was a preacher who traveled around, sharing the gospel. His mother, Clara, worked as a chiropractor while also taking care of Jim and his three siblings on their family farm. As a young boy, Jim loved building model ships and airplanes, reading, and collecting postage stamps. He had a talent in art, and one elementary school teacher loved his work so much that she used Jim's drawings to decorate her classroom.

As he moved into high school, he discovered a talent for acting and giving speeches. But he was especially known for carrying his Bible everywhere he went, praying before lunch, and jumping at every chance to talk with others about Jesus. After school, Jim had chores: feeding chickens, rabbits, and goats; running errands; and doing yard work. He learned to work hard and help his family, and he put that work ethic to use in helping his older brother with a garbage-collecting business.

Jim had an adventurous spirit, and he and his friends often hitchhiked around Oregon on camping and hunting expeditions. On one of these trips, one of his friends was climbing over a fence to find a buzzard he had shot when he accidentally pulled his rifle's trigger. The bullet grazed Jim's head, going through his hair. Just a tiny bit lower and it would have killed him. This was one of three near-death experiences Jim went through.

After high school, Jim went off to Wheaton College in Illinois. He joined the wrestling team and participated in the college's missionary society. The next summer, Jim and a friend hitchhiked to Mexico, where the friend's parents were missionaries. This trip convinced Jim that he was meant to be a missionary. He wrote about the trip in his journal:

> The Lord has been good to me in bringing me here and giving this brief

opportunity to see the field and hear the language a bit. Missionaries are very human folks, just doing what they are asked. Simply a bunch of nobodies trying to exalt Somebody.

When he returned to school, Jim began studying Greek. He wanted to learn to read the New Testament in its original language, believing this would help him translate it into new languages as a missionary. But his time wasn't spent just studying for class. He kept lists of people to pray for and would do so as he walked to class or waited in line for meals. He also used these times to memorize Bible verses, which he kept on small cards in his pockets. From a young age, Jim seemed to understand that life was short and each moment needed to be used wisely.

One day, Jim and some friends were traveling in a car on a mission to share the gospel. As they crossed some railroad tracks, the car stalled. Unable to get it started again, the passengers all jumped out mere seconds before a train crashed into the car, demolishing it. Writing to his parents about the wreck, he said, "It sobered me considerably to think that the Lord kept me from harm in this. Certainly He has a work that He wants me in somewhere." This was his second scrape with death.

It was around this time that Jim met a friend's sister named Elisabeth. The more time he spent with her, the more he liked her. But he wasn't sure that God wanted him to be married. Knowing he was meant to go to another country as a missionary, Jim was concerned that marriage might distract him from his mission for God. He wanted to serve his Savior with every part of himself. So he and Betty (short for Elisabeth) committed their relationship to God, choosing not to spend much time together and instead praying that God would bring them together if that was His plan.

Friends and family members didn't understand many of Jim's choices. At times he struggled to find friends who thought like he did. Many people thought he and Betty should just get married, and his family wondered why he wanted to go to another country when there was work to do for God in the United States. But Jim knew he needed to seek God's approval, not man's.

After college, Jim spent time at home, helping his family and teaching others about God at every opportunity. He also spent a lot of time praying about his future. He knew he would go to another country, but didn't know where. Two opportunities came up: one to go to India and another to go to Ecuador. Unsure which to choose, he trusted that God would make it clear in His timing. In the meantime, Jim continued to serve Him faithfully by teaching in churches and after-school Bible studies for kids.

Jim met a former missionary to Ecuador, who told him about the Quichuas, who lived in the jungle there. The missionary also told Jim about a tribe they called the "Aucas." These people had never been reached by the outside world. They were a violent group who killed any who dared to contact them, including Quichuas and white men. Jim's adventurous spirit kicked in, and he began to dream about reaching these people with the gospel. He set aside ten days to pray and seek God's wisdom to determine if He was leading him to Ecuador. Through his time reading the Bible and talking with God, Jim received the answer to his prayer. He would join the work in Ecuador.

With that decided, Jim set about gathering what he needed for his journey to South America. In early 1952, he and a friend set off on a ship from San Pedro, California. Twenty days later, they arrived at their port in Ecuador and joined up with another missionary. The first task was learning Spanish. Jim was quick to pick up the language, but not as quick as he wanted to be. He was anxious to be able to talk to people about Jesus and frustrated that they couldn't understand him. His heart was drawn more and more to the Auca people, but he knew he had to learn Spanish and the Quichua language before he could hope to understand the language of this hidden tribe.

Jim knew he would learn the language and customs of the Ecuadorian people best by spending time with them, so he traveled around with Spanish-speaking guides, going to bullfights and climbing mountains. He wanted to practice his Spanish every chance he got. Elisabeth also made her way to Ecuador, where she worked to learn Spanish and occasionally got to see Jim, although they were working in different places much of the time.

Soon, Jim flew to a jungle outpost to see the work with the Quichuas and plan where he would live. He had heard that some Quichuas had been able to make friendly contact with the Aucas, but this turned out to be untrue. The Aucas had just killed five Quichuas in that area. Jim wrote in a letter to his younger sister, "It would take a miracle to open the way to [the Aucas], and we are praying for that miracle. They may be only a few hundred in number, but they are a part of the whole creation, and we have orders for such." He took the Great Commission of Matthew 28 seriously—they were to go into the world and preach to all nations. And Revelation 7:9 says people from every tongue would worship Jesus. So Jim believed he must make every effort to share the gospel with the Auca tribe.

As Jim spent time in prayer and reading the Bible, he wrote in his journal, "I recognized that all I am and have is the Almighty's. He could in one instant change the whole course of my life—with accident, tragedy, or any event unforeseen." Jim believed that, whatever happened to him, "what God does is well done." He trusted God with his life, no matter what.

In the jungle, one of Jim's main tasks was setting up a village for the missionaries. He worked all day with the Quichuas, building houses, a school, and a clinic. But then heavy rains came, and the ground started to fall away into the river below the village. As Jim and his friend, Pete, worked to carry equipment out of the destroyed buildings and into the jungle, more and more land was washing away. At one point, Jim was standing on the side of a building where the earth was washing away, and suddenly he heard a loud roar. He looked, and all the ground around him had fallen away. The Quichuas, who couldn't see him, shouted, "He dies!" But the small bit of land where Jim stood remained, and he yelled back, "I live!" Once again, God had spared Jim Elliot's life.

The building work had to be started again, but first, at the age of twenty-six, Jim and Elisabeth were finally married. They worked together in translation and teaching, and the first several months of their marriage were spent in a tent. As the people in the jungle began to trust Jesus for salvation, Jim trained them to begin preaching to and teaching their own people. He and Betty welcomed a daughter, Valerie, to their jungle home. Their missionary life had challenges, but it was good. They were working with friends and seeing people come to know Christ.

One day, two of Jim's fellow missionaries, Ed McCully and Nate Saint, were flying over the jungle when they spotted Auca houses. They came back and shared their excitement with Jim, who was thrilled. Ed and Nate began flying around these homes, using a bucket and rope to drop gifts to the people below. Jim learned some Auca phrases from a girl who had come from their tribe years before. He joined Nate in the plane and, using a loudspeaker, shouted in the Auca language, "We are your friends," and other messages. The Aucas gave gifts in return. Maybe they weren't as savage as others said. Maybe they didn't kill all white people for sport. Perhaps through these gifts, the door was opening for Jim and the others to learn the Auca language and bring the gospel to them.

The men came up with a plan to land their plane on the beach near the Auca homes. As they made preparations, Jim wrote in a letter:

> We would like to reach this tribe. They have never had friendly contact either with whites or Indians, but we know where they live and will make a definite effort to reach them soon. This needs two things. The first is secrecy. There are some who, if they got wind of our

plan, could wreck the whole deal, so don't tell this to anyone till I write you to do so. The second thing is prayer. These people are killers and have no idea of getting along with outsiders. Our Indians are deathly afraid of them, as are the whites, and we will be called fools for our pains, but we believe that God has brought Ed to Arajuno [the village closest to the Auca homes] for this contact and we want to do His will in taking the gospel to them. They have no word for God in their language, let alone a word for Jesus.

Finally, the thing Jim had been praying about for years was going to happen. They were going to go to the Aucas. Jim, Ed, Nate, Pete, and another missionary, named Roger, flew out on January 4, 1956. Jim wrote Betty from their spot on what they called "Palm Beach." They had landed and built a treehouse so they could be off the ground. He wrote, "Our hopes are up but no signs of the 'neighbors' yet. Perhaps today is the day the Aucas will be reached."

Two days later, a man and two women walked out of the jungle and onto the beach where the five missionaries waited. These three curious Aucas ate the food they were offered—hamburgers, lemonade, mustard. They rubbed bug spray on their skin, gaining instant relief from the constant mosquito bites. They tried to communicate, but neither group could understand the other. The Auca man, whom the missionaries called "George," wanted to go up in the airplane. So, Nate took him for a flight. Back on the beach, the missionaries used models and hand motions to try to explain that they wanted to clear an airstrip so the plane could come and land there more often. But it was too difficult—the Aucas couldn't possibly understand.

After a while, George and the women walked back into the jungle. They returned to their people, full of things to tell them.

The next day, Jim and the other men waited eagerly for the Aucas to return. They didn't.

The following morning, Sunday, the men woke, and Nate took the plane up to scout things out. He saw around ten Aucas heading toward the missionaries. He quickly landed the plane and shouted the news to the others. He used a radio to tell his wife they were expecting visitors soon and to be near the radio again at 4:30 that afternoon for a report.

The five men sang together as they waited for the Aucas to arrive.

At 4:30, no one called the women on the radio. All five men had been speared by the Aucas, and their bodies were later found by a rescue crew sent to recover them.

Jim Elliot, who had been spared from death three times, was now dead.

Jim gave his life for these people, fully knowing the risks in trying to contact them but believing the opportunity was worth those risks. God used his death, and the deaths of the other four men, to show the world the treasure of the gospel. As news spread of their murders, many people thought it was senseless—why had these men risked their lives?

But for Jim, it wasn't senseless; it made all the sense in the world. He firmly believed what he had written years before: "He is no fool who gives what he cannot keep to gain what he cannot lose."

Jim's wife, Elisabeth, stayed in Ecuador, waiting for an opportunity to reach the Aucas. It came, and she and her daughter moved into the village to work with the Waorani people, as she came to know them. (Auca was the Quichua word for savage, but the people called themselves Waorani.)

Shortly after Jim's death, Elisabeth told a friend, "The fact that Jesus Christ died for all makes me interested in the salvation of all, but the fact that Jim loved and died for the Aucas intensifies my love for them." Because of his love for them, Elisabeth was able to share the gospel with them, and many believed and became Jim's brothers and sisters in Christ.

SOURCE

Elisabeth Elliot, *Shadow of the Almighty: The Life and Testimony of Jim Elliot* (New York: Harper Collins, 1989).

Elisabeth Elliot, *The Savage My Kinsman* (Ann Arbor, MI: Servant Books, 1989).

Strength in Love

Jim Elliot was just twenty-eight when he died. He and the other men who went to "Palm Beach" knew the danger. They didn't have to go. Many people thought it was reckless for them to leave their wives and children and put their lives at risk. Why did they do it?

Jim believed God had put a love for the Auca people in his heart and had led him to this point. Knowing that God loved them and that they had no knowledge of Him compelled Jim to do whatever it took to bring them the gospel message. He was willing to die for these people because he

171

knew Jesus had died for them, and he knew that in death he would gain something far greater than he could even imagine.

Sometimes sacrificial love looks like what Jim did. In fact, the greatest example we have of sacrificial love comes from Jesus, who died to save His enemies. He sacrificed everything for our sake, becoming a human child, experiencing sickness and pain and temptation, and dying a cruel death on the cross. There is no greater love.

But sacrificial love doesn't always mean physical death. Most of the time, it means dying to ourselves, one day at a time, putting aside what we want so we can love others well. The decision Jim made to risk his life didn't come in an instant; it was the result of a lifetime of small decisions to sacrifice his own comfort for the sake of others.

For you, these small decisions might be letting someone else choose what game to play or what movie to watch. It might mean letting someone go in front of you in line. Or it could mean risking your reputation with your friends in order to befriend a new kid. Anytime you give up something for someone else, you're showing sacrificial love.

But this love doesn't come naturally—it's a fruit of the Spirit, which means God grows it in you as you spend time with Him, reading the Bible, praying, and worshiping Him. What might look like weakness to other people—giving up something for someone else—is actually only possible with God's strength. The same God who gave Jim amazing sacrificial love for others can do the same for you. Just ask Him.

Questions

1. Read Romans 5:5–8. What has been poured into our hearts through the Holy Spirit?

2. According to verses 7 and 8, how is God's love different from our love? How did He prove His love?

3. Whom in your life do you struggle to love well? Why do you think it's so hard?

4. While we're still living in this world, struggling with sin, we'll never love perfectly. But we do have opportunities to show sacrificial love to others. Can you think of any times you've seen someone (or even yourself) sacrifice for someone else?

5. Movies and books are full of examples of this kind of love. Can you think of any stories of characters who have sacrificed their lives for someone else? These stories are shadows that can point us to the ultimate sacrifice of Jesus. How is His sacrifice better?

LOVE consists in this:
not that we loved God,
but that **HE LOVED US**
and sent his Son to be
the atoning **SACRIFICE**
for our sins. Dear
friends, if **GOD** loved
us in this way, we
also **MUST** love one
another.
–1 John 4:10–11

"I believe that what I did was done for me— that **MY FAITH IN GOD SUSTAINED ME** in my fight."

Jackie Robinson
ENDURANCE

Jack ("Jackie") Roosevelt Robinson, was born January 31, 1919, at his family home in Cairo, Georgia. He was the youngest of five children, and his parents, Jerry and Mallie Robinson, lived on a plantation where they worked hard for little money. To survive, Mallie had to make a deal for them to work as sharecroppers, which meant they would farm some of the plantation land, but could only keep half of the crops. She was a strong woman with a strong faith, and she raised her family to work hard with the God-given talent and energy they had.

When Jackie was six months old, his father abandoned the family. Mallie and the children were forced to move off the plantation, and she decided they should move far away from the growing racism of Georgia, where many African Americans were being treated with violence. So, when Jackie was one year old, they moved to California.

Mallie worked hard in their new hometown of Pasadena. She was able to buy a home, which happened to be in an all-white neighborhood. Many neighbors didn't want the Robinsons to live there, but she persisted in serving and loving the neighbors until many became her friends.

Growing up, Jackie learned from his mother to be proud of his color, heritage, and culture. She taught her children that God wanted them to be black and that it was a good thing. She also taught them about her faith in God and had them in church every week. But as a young teenager, Jackie was more interested in sports and hanging out with friends than he was in church or in God. But then the church got a new pastor, Reverend Karl Downs.

Karl Downs was just seven years older than Jackie, and he recognized that Jackie was a leader. He wanted to get young people interested in the church, so he got Jackie to help him. Jackie started spending more time at the church building, teaching Sunday school and telling younger boys about God.

Jackie later wrote about what Karl Downs had taught him, including the following lessons:

> Not only to stay out of evil—but to try to get into good.
> To seek to help others without thinking so much of what we will get out of it, but what we are putting into it.

These lessons followed Jackie throughout his life, and they helped him make important choices that would change American culture.

But there were challenges to being a black man, and Jackie was known for his temper and desire to fight when he was treated badly. He was once arrested for standing up to a white man who had called Jackie and his friends an evil word. Proud of his skin color, he wanted everyone else to recognize his value and worth, and he reacted in anger when he was treated badly.

In his college years at UCLA, Jackie excelled at football, basketball, track and field, and baseball. Actually, although he would one day be

world-famous for his skill at baseball, in college
it was his worst sport. He quit college in his
senior year, anxious to get a job and support his
mother. He worked a few different jobs and even
played semiprofessional football in Hawaii while
working a construction job near Pearl Harbor.
On December 5, 1941, Jackie left Hawaii to start
a new job in Los Angeles, California. Two days
later, the Japanese bombed Pearl Harbor and the
United States entered World War II.

Knowing he would probably be called to fight
in the war, Jackie wanted to fight for freedom for
those being persecuted by Japan and Germany.
But he also saw a problem with America asking
African Americans to fight for freedom on the
other side of the world when they weren't given
freedom and equal rights in their own country.
When he entered the army in March 1942, he
quickly rose through the ranks and became an
officer. But even then, he was treated badly at
times because of the color of his skin. He had to
ride in the back of the bus, was told he had to play

on the black baseball team on his military base, and had to drink out of a different water fountain than white soldiers.

When he left the army in 1944, he began playing baseball for the Kansas City Monarchs, part of a league for just black players. At the time, there were no African Americans in Major League Baseball. They had to play in their own league. Jackie did well enough to later try out for the Boston Red Sox. But while the Red Sox allowed black players to try out, they had no interest in letting them join the team. Jackie went back to playing for the Monarchs, where his batting average (how often he hit the ball) was .345 (a normal average is around .250 or .275). This made Jackie an All-Star. But his temper often got him in trouble, and he was known for fighting with umpires, teammates, and players on the other teams. After a few seasons with the Monarchs, Jackie decided to quit, move back to California, and marry his girlfriend, Rachel.

But then Branch Rickey, president of the Brooklyn Dodgers, met with Jackie Robinson on an August morning in 1945. He asked if Jackie would be interested in breaking the color barrier in baseball by becoming the first African American to play on a major-league team.

In this meeting, Branch Rickey read Jesus' words from the Sermon on the Mount to Jackie, which says, "You have heard that it was said, An eye for an eye and a tooth for a tooth. But I tell you, don't resist an evildoer. On the contrary, if anyone slaps you on your right cheek, turn the other to him also" (Matthew 5:38–39).

Jackie responded, "I have two cheeks, Mr. Rickey. Is that it?"

Rickey nodded. He knew Jackie would face many trials and would have to turn the other cheek instead of fighting back if they were going to have success in bringing African American players into Major League Baseball. If he fought back, people would say he had a temper and would claim he and other black players didn't belong in *the league.* It wouldn't be easy or fair, but Rickey believed this was the only way it would work.

After thinking about it, Jackie agreed to join Rickey in desegregating baseball. He spent his first season with the Dodgers' minor-league team, based in Montreal, Canada. He knew the huge responsibility he had taken on, saying, "I will not forget that I am representing a whole race of people who are pulling for me." But challenges began in spring training, which was held in Florida, where Jim Crow laws put Jackie's life in danger. His wife was afraid he would try to fight those mistreating them and would be killed for it. From the airport to hotels to buses to ballparks, strangers made it clear that Jackie and Rachel did not have the same rights as white people.

But it wasn't only the danger of racism that made life hard for Jackie. He also had the pressure of being a leader for millions of African Americans whose hopes were resting on him. If he succeeded, they would succeed. If he failed, they would fail. Huge crowds of both white and black baseball fans came to watch his games. While many cities in Florida refused to let him play in their ballparks, Jackie survived spring training and traveled with the team to Jersey City, New Jersey, for their first regular-season game.

In his second time at bat, Jackie hit a home run, bringing home two runners. He ended the game with four hits, four runs scored, and two stolen bases. Soon, he was leading the minor league in batting average. Montreal's fans loved him, but he faced hatred in many American cities. Fans and other players yelled terrible things at him during games. Pitchers threw balls at his head, and players slid into him on purpose as he guarded second base. But Jackie continued to turn the other cheek, controlling his urge to fight back. At the end of the season, Montreal won the championship, and Jackie was carried away from the dressing room by a group of Canadian fans. He loved the fans in Montreal, saying, "They inspired me and, along with the faith I had in God, who was on my side right from opening day of the season, I had a wonderful year."

The next season, having proved himself in the minor league, Jackie started with the Brooklyn Dodgers in the major league. The pressure was on more than ever. It wasn't enough to just be good; he had to be great in order to prove that African Americans belonged in the league. On April 15, 1947, Jackie became the first black player to play in Major League Baseball since the 1880s, when a man named Moses Walker played one season. He welcomed the challenge, but a week later, in Philadelphia, he experienced the worst treatment yet from the Phillies players. They yelled horrible things at him every time he stepped up to the plate to bat. Tired and angry, Jackie wanted to fight back and quit baseball. But he stood in the batter's box, and his teammates began to rally around him.

One teammate, Ralph Branca, invited Jackie to dinner and asked him, "How do you just sit silently and take it?"

Jackie responded, "Ralph, many nights I get down on my knees and pray to God for the strength not to fight back."

That strength helped Jackie and the Dodgers win the National League pennant, making them one of the two best teams in the league that year. Fans all over America were inspired by his quiet strength. Both black and white boys imitated him on baseball fields, and parents named their children after him.

One day, Jackie received a letter from a man who had met a little black boy named Jimmy. Jimmy had told him that he wished he was white. So, the man asked Jackie to write a letter to Jimmy. Jackie wrote Jimmy, encouraging him to keep his faith in God and be glad for how he was made. He wrote, "Look in the mirror at yourself and be proud of what God gave you. I, too, felt the pains you must feel, but I never have been ashamed of what God has given me."

After Jackie had played a few seasons, Branch Rickey gave Jackie permission to speak up when he was treated badly. Through his skill on the field and his humility, he had earned respect, and people listened to him. He was living out what his mother had taught him: "God wants human beings to work and speak for the freedom and equality which is rightfully theirs, even if they must suffer because they do this." He also spoke about his faith more and how it was prayer that helped him not to fight back.

After ten years in the league, Jackie retired from baseball and began working and speaking for civil rights and equality. Martin Luther King Jr. often said Jackie had inspired him to stand up and seek freedom and equal rights for all Americans. He said of Jackie, "He was a sit-inner before the sit-ins, a freedom rider before the freedom rides."

Through the rest of his life, Jackie used his fame and reputation to seek the good of others. He wrote to presidents, asking them to help seek justice. He gave money to civil rights groups, started companies to help people, and wrote his opinions in a weekly newspaper column.

When he died in 1972, more than 2,500 people came to his funeral. Thousands more stood along the streets as his body was taken to the cemetery.

People wanted to pay respect to the man who had stood against hatred and had changed America.

In the cemetery where his body is buried in Brooklyn, New York, Jackie Robinson's tombstone spells out what he believed was the godly purpose of his life: "A life is not important except in the impact it has on other lives."

SOURCE

Michael G. Long and Chris Lamb, *Jackie Robinson: A Spiritual Biography: The Faith of a Boundary-Breaking Hero* (Louisville, KY: Westminster John Knox Press, 2017).

Strength in Endurance

Every year on April 15, Major League Baseball holds "Jackie Robinson Day." Teams honor the stand Jackie made and his courage under such hard circumstances. It's hard for us to imagine a time when sports leagues were segregated, but this day reminds us that it took the strength of men like Jackie Robinson and Branch Rickey to make that change.

What we don't always hear about is Jackie's faith in God, which led him to take on this challenge, and his dependence on God, which gave him the strength to stand firm when he faced insults and injuries because of the color of his skin. Jackie looked to Jesus as an example and trusted God to take care of him. He knew the truth that all people are created in God's image, and he lived his life to teach that truth to other people.

The same God who gave Jackie the strength to stand up for truth can strengthen you. The Savior, Jesus, who turned the other cheek, can help you trust Him when you suffer for doing what is right.

This doesn't mean you should just accept it when people treat you or others badly. Both by his silence and his speech, Jackie showed the injustice of racism. God can give you the strength to stand in the same way. Remember, you can always ask Him for help—He loves to help His children.

Questions

1. After Jesus preached that we should turn the other cheek, He talked about how we should treat enemies. Read Matthew 5:43. What do some people say we should do to our enemies?

2. Look at the next verse, Matthew 5:44. What does Jesus say we should do to our enemies?

3. How did Jesus live out these words? (Hint: See what He said on the cross in Luke 23:34.)

4. Have you ever had an opportunity to choose between loving and hating your enemies? What was that like?

5. Jesus also said we should pray for those who persecute us. What do you think we should pray for? Should we just pray that they will be kind, or is there more for which we should pray? Spend some time praying now—for those who are unkind and for the strength to love them and to persevere in doing good.

Rejoice in **HOPE**; be patient in affliction; be **PERSISTENT** in prayer.—Romans 12:12

Alvin York

Born December 13, 1887; Died September 2, 1964

Grew up in a small town in the hills of Tennessee, where he worked on the family farm

Was known as one of the best shooters around, but when World War I began, he hoped he wouldn't be called to fight because he believed it was wrong

Was called into the Army and traveled to Germany, where in one battle he captured 132 German soldiers

Came home a war hero and used his fame and money to build schools for children in his hometown

George Müller

Born September 27, 1805; Died March 10, 1898

Spent his childhood and teenage years stealing and gambling before his life was changed by God when he began attending prayer meetings

Became a pastor, and was sad to see poor children unable to go to school in his town

Opened schools for orphans, depending on God to provide money, clothing, and food for his family and the children in the schools

In his lifetime, his schools cared for more than ten thousand children.

Dietrich Bonhoeffer

Born February 4, 1906; Died April 9, 1945

Lived in Germany during World War I and World War II

As a German pastor, he went against many fellow pastors who followed Adolf Hitler, believing it was more important to follow the teachings of Jesus than to gain political power.

Became a double agent, working secretly to try to stop Hitler

Was arrested and held in prison for two years before being killed

 # Brother Andrew

Born May 11, 1928

Fought in the Dutch army in Indonesia

Earned the nickname "God's Smuggler" by secretly taking Bibles into Communist countries

Has traveled to more than 125 countries

In 1981, he and a team smuggled one million Bibles into China in one mission.

Started Open Doors, an organization that helps persecuted Christians around the world

Elka of the Wai Wai

Born around 1933

Lived as a chief and witch doctor in the jungles of Guyana and Brazil

Gave up his powers to follow Jesus, even when everyone in his village expected him to die for it

Became a pastor, preaching to his tribe and helping translate the Bible into their language

He and his fellow Christians traveled to other villages to tell people about Jesus, becoming jungle missionaries.

Eric Liddell

Born January 16, 1902; Died February 21, 1945

Won a gold medal in the 400-meter race for the United Kingdom in the 1924 Olympic Games in Paris

Refusing to run on Sundays, he gave up the chance to run in one of his best races, the 100-meter dash

After the Olympics, he moved to China to be a missionary.

During World War II, he was placed in a Chinese "internment camp," much like a prison. He died there of a brain tumor, and was mourned by all his fellow prisoners who had loved and respected him deeply.

John Newton

Born July 24, 1725; Died December 21, 1807

Went on his first voyage as a sailor when he was eleven

As an adult, became the captain of a slave ship that transported kidnapped slaves from Africa to the Caribbean and America

Became a Christian and, later, a pastor and hymn writer. His hymn "Amazing Grace" is one of the most recorded songs of all time

His testimony about the treatment of slaves on slave ships helped lead to the abolition of the British slave trade

William Carey

Born August 17, 1761; Died June 9, 1834

As a child, he loved maps and stories about explorers

Became a pastor in England, but longed to move to a place where he could preach to people who had never heard of Jesus

Started a missionary society in England that sent him to India, where he built schools and translated the Bible into many languages

Is known as the "Father of Modern Missions" because his teaching and writing influenced many missionaries to go around the world and share the gospel

George Liele

Born 1750; Died 1820

Grew up as a slave in Virginia, and later, Georgia

Became a Christian in the local Baptist church, and became the first ordained African American Baptist pastor in America

Was the first American missionary, moving to Jamaica to preach and spread the gospel message

Played a role in the abolition of the British slave trade

Jim Elliot

Born October 8, 1927; Died January 8, 1956

A mission trip to Mexico in college convinced him that he should be a missionary

Moved to Ecuador, where he worked with the Quichua people, teaching them about Jesus

Worked to find a way to reach a tribe that had never heard of Jesus

With other missionary friends, was killed on the beach by this tribe. Later, his wife and daughter moved to the jungle to live and share God's love with the people who had killed him.

Jackie Robinson

Born January 31, 1919; Died October 24, 1972

Grew up in California, where he excelled at football, basketball, track and field, and baseball

Played baseball in a league for African American players, gaining attention from Branch Rickey, the president of the MLB's Brooklyn Dodgers

Became the first African American to play in Major League Baseball in the modern era.

Faced persecution, violence, and insults, and relied on the Lord in prayer to persevere

ALSO
AVAILABLE!